EX LIBRIS

LEOPOLD CLASSIC LIBRARY

LILLIAN WHITING

THE WORLD BEAUTIFUL. SECOND SERIES

LEOPOLD CLASSIC LIBRARY

Leopold Classic Library is delighted to publish this classic book as part of our extensive collection. As part of our on-going commitment to delivering value to the reader, we have also provided you with a link to a website, where you may download a digital version of this work for free.

Free download of this book is available here:
http://tinyurl.com/leopold-worldbeautiful03whitgoog

Many of the books in our collection have been out of print for decades, and therefore have not been accessible to the general public. Whilst the books in this collection have not been hand curated, an aim of our publishing program is to facilitate rapid access to this vast reservoir of literature. As a result of this book being first published many decades ago, it may have occasional imperfections. These imperfections may include poor picture quality, blurred or missing text. While some of these imperfections may have appeared in the original work, others may have resulted from the scanning process that has been applied. However, our view is that this is a significant literary work, which deserves to be brought back into print after many decades. While some publishers have applied optical character recognition (OCR), this approach has its own drawbacks, which include formatting errors, misspelt words, or the presence of inappropriate characters. Our philosophy has been guided by a desire to provide the reader with an experience that is as close as possible to ownership of the original work. We hope that you will enjoy this wonderful classic book, and that the occasional imperfection that it might contain will not detract from the experience.

THE WORLD BEAUTIFUL. SECOND SERIES

THE

WORLD BEAUTIFUL.

Second Series.

BY

LILIAN WHITING,

AUTHOR OF

"THE WORLD BEAUTIFUL" (FIRST SERIES),
AND "FROM DREAMLAND SENT."

But what is land, or what is wave,
To me who only jewels crave?
EMERSON.

BOSTON:

LITTLE, BROWN, AND COMPANY.

1911.

TO

CHARLES GORDON AMES,

Minister of the Church of the Disciples,

AND

FANNY B. AMES,

WHOSE LIVES ENRICH AND EXALT THE WORLD IN WHICH
THEY LIVE,

These papers are inscribed by

LILIAN WHITING.

"I will wait heaven's perfect hour
Through the innumerable years."

CONTENTS.

Vibrations.

The Unseen World.

THE WORLD BEAUTIFUL.

" According to the power that worketh in you."

THE WORLD BEAUTIFUL.

SYMPATHETIC SOCIAL RELATIONS.

GOOD society, the best society, is none too good for any honest Christian man or woman to enter, and of which to form an integral part; but its claim to be called the best must be tested by the ideals to which it holds itself amenable, by the ends it pursues, by its sympathy with all humanity.

Life gains in proportion as it is responsive and sympathetic. A human being is not a machine. Fixed hours and correspondingly fixed duties are all very well as a necessity, but at best they are the mere frame-work of living and not life itself. The ideal life is that which has its freedom, its easy elasticity, its large possibilities of inclusiveness; and where these can be attained and commanded, so much the better. Work is made for people, but people are not made for work, in the sense of severe restriction.

The highest ideal of happiness lies in social intercourse; the highest luxury of life lies in a sympathetic relation to one's fellow-beings. This involves time : but can time be better used? Professor Drummond, in "The Greatest Thing in the World," calls particular attention to the fact that so much of the time of Jesus was spent simply in doing kind things. "To love abundantly is to live abundantly." To live in those easy, cordial relations that promote love and good-will is to reach the highest standpoint in human experience. He who puts the most into life, of generous and outgiving sympathies and interests, gets the most out of life. He may end his days with less money earned or made, but he holds treasure of a more permanent and a more satisfying nature.

To leave undone those things which we

ought to do, to leave unspoken the word of recognition or appreciation that we should have said, is perhaps as positive a wrong as it is to do the thing we should not have done. We talk of success as an aim of life ; but what better form can it take than that of easy and sympathetic relation with every one with whom we have to do ? Social relations are not the mere amusements or even enjoyments of life, but are an integral part of its conduct. " The essential element in life is conduct," well says Bishop Spalding ; and it is hardly too much to say that the essential element in conduct is that of the loves, the friendships, the personal attractions and sympathies that govern the course of general life as inevitably as the tides follow the moon or the stars pursue their orbits. There is a vast amount, however, of sufficiently agreeable and amiable social inter-course which passes current for friendship, that has in it no staying power, that is not under any intelligent or controlled direction, but is at the chance of every tide and im-pulse, or of popular sentiment. This amiable

mutual intercourse may exist for years, for
half a lifetime or more, flowing on smoothly,
and its undisturbed shallowness may be mistaken for depth, until some vital impulse
enters into the life of one, and then the
depth of this amiable understanding is suddenly tested. Whether it is genuine or not is
swiftly revealed. The test sooner or later
comes into every life.

> " I hung my verses in the wind,
>   Time and tide their faults may find.
>   All were winnowed through and through,
>   Five lines lasted sound and true;
>   Five were smelted in a pot
>   Than the South more fierce and hot;
>   These the siroc could not melt
>   Fire their fiercer flaming felt.
>   And the meaning was more white
>   Than July's meridian light.
>   Sunshine cannot bleach the snow,
>   Nor time unmake what poets know.
>   Have you eyes to find the five
>   Which five hundred did survive ? "

This is the typical test, applied not only
to the poet's expression, but to every other
form of the expressions of life. Every pro-

fessed and alleged feeling must sometime be
" winnowed through and through." It must
survive the fire or be melted away with the
refuse.

There is one form of discrimination that
friendships take, which arrogates to itself a
high moral basis, and yet which is perhaps
more untrue to any genuine ideal faith than
any other aspect of its deflection. To ignore
friends because of external differences, as a
change from wealth to poverty or anything of
that kind, is a vulgarity to which the refined
nature could not stoop. Quite aside from
ethics or emotion, the very culture and refinement of a refined and cultured individual
would effectually obviate this form of deflection from any social relation. But the subtler
current allies itself with what one pleases to
call his moral nature, and assumes the form of
a moral judgment.

There are tragic complications in life that
suddenly descend at times like a whirlwind
and envelop a group of people in the most unforeseen and startling manner. They all be-

come, perforce, actors in a tragedy. They can
no more escape their individual rôles than
could the wayfarer on the plains escape a
storm that descends from the heavens without
an instant's warning. What then? Ah, this
is *the test*. To the actors immediately concerned it is the tragedy; to all their social
circle it is the test. The manner in which this
test brings out latent and perhaps hitherto un-
suspected qualities offers an interesting study,
indeed, of human nature. There will, of
course, be those who sweepingly and crudely
proclaim their belief, or disbelief, in certain
things. There will be those who unhesitatingly condemn; those who as unhesitatingly
uphold and sustain. The majority of friends
and acquaintances range themselves on one
side, as they are pleased to term it, or the other.
And it is just this "taking sides," whether
it be with an undiscriminating faith that is
well-nigh credulity, or with an equally undiscriminating condemnation, — it is just this
"taking sides" which is not a just or true
act in friendship ideally considered. To de-

cide that one's friend has certainly done wrong, that there is no room for doubt, and that, *ergo*, the friendship is at an end, — is not to stand the test. To espouse the "side" one believes is right, to condemn the "side" he believes is wrong, is not to stand the test. What then? Shall one condone or tacitly uphold what he knows is error?

By no means. But any friendship worthy the name is large enough to include each and all, — those who have sinned, those who have been sinned against. Human life, as impersonated in each individual, is made up of mingled imperfections, striving with more or less genuineness and ardor for perfection. Friendship should mean sympathy and support to all such striving ; it should mean charitable and tender comprehension of wrong, and sympathetic aid in leading it toward the right. The attitude that "So-and-so has erred ; it is unmistakably clear ; henceforth our friendship is at an end" — is the attitude of a barbarian, of a savage, of the most untaught and unreflecting character. It is an attitude unworthy of any intelligent, not to say high-minded, individual.

The divine reconcilement includes the universal attitude of sympathy, of aid, of love. "Leave there thy gift before the altar *and go and be reconciled to thy brother;* then come and offer thy gift."

It is the law and the prophets.

A conviction is sometimes held that a busy life, and a life whose days are filled with little kindnesses, must necessarily be two different experiences, instead of being identical. To be "engaged in a special work" implies, it would sometimes seem, a complete emancipation on the part of the worker from the ordinary amenities and courtesies of life. On a superficial view there may seem to be a reason for this. Special work requires special conditions. The painter, the poet, and the prophet must have his periods of solitude with which the world intermeddleth not. He cannot be at the mercy of accidents. If he has set out to accomplish a certain work, it is his duty, his divine obligation, to achieve it.

Secondly, there is a kind of traditional belief that almost any one can be kind and
thoughtful, and that, indeed, the person whose
time is of no particular value is the one of all
others especially appointed to be of service
to other people.

But is not this the deeper truth, that the one
most helpful in small things is the one best
fitted to accomplish a great work ?   The lives
of the greatest people substantiate this theory.
There is no living man who has accomplished
so much in so many different ways as Mr.
Gladstone.   Because he was a statesman,
with the care of an Empire on his mind, did
not hinder him from the scholar's joy in
classical reading and extended translation, nor
from his constant attendance on religious
rites, often performing the duties of a lay
service, nor from the daily and hourly manifestations, countless in number, of courtesies,
kindnesses, benefactions to his family, and his
widely extended social relationships.   Mrs.
Livermore, whose grandeur of character is
pre-eminently conceded by the entire coun-

try, is another signal instance of the great
individual who is so swift in response to
every human need, to every social courtesy,
to every friendly obligation, that to the superficial observer it would appear that even all
her time was insufficient to so scrupulously answer every letter; to speak the kind word, to do
the generous act, — yet with all these details,
her great work is being successfully conducted
to noble issues.   The unmistakable inference
is that when one places himself thus in the
highest thought currents — in the currents of
the most generous and the most intense spiritual life — the miracle is wrought, and time
is multiplied as were the loaves and the
fishes.

There is philosophy as well as philanthropy
in the keeping in touch with all sweetness
and love; in the being swift to be kind.
This is living on the spiritual plane, and
spirituality is power.   It is the most infinite
potency.   "Seek ye *first* the kingdom of
Heaven," — that is, this kingdom of spiritual
power, — "and all things shall be added unto

you." To the degree in which one is swiftly
responsive and constantly in touch with love,
and generosity, and kindness, and thoughtful
consideration, to that degree does he command
the potencies of life. He is living as a spirit,
in the spiritual world, and among spiritual
forces. To the degree in which he is selfish
and unsympathetic, to that degree is he
dwelling on a low plane, in a lower and
cruder order of life. It is as if one should
crouch and crawl when he might stand firm
and walk uprightly. Or as if he should
choose to walk in alleys or over rough stones
instead of on noble boulevards with radiant
and enchanting views. The moment one asserts his true dignity of life as a spiritual
being, essentially, although temporarily dwelling amid the scenery of the physical world,
that moment does he begin to live on a plane
where he holds mastery over conditions.

There is much talk in the air over thought
centres and thought currents. "The great
dual principle of this world is love and wisdom; and the latter can only be developed

through the former. The intellect is entirely
dependent upon the affections." The initial
step is always tranquillity. No human being
can live in this world of conflicts within and
conflicts without and not at times feel a burn-
ing sense of injustice and irritation. All that
must be eliminated. Wrong must be forgiven,
and the mind and heart filled with impulses
of love and sweetness. The divine injunction
to *love* your enemies, to pray for those who
despitefully use you, must be fulfilled to the
most entire and complete extent. Then having cast out all that is fretful and jarring,
one may open his mind to the angelic influences. Prayer is simply occult activity, — the
intensest form of spiritual life. Praying for
the divine impulse to enter, it will come.
One will be filled with peace and joy. He
will find his true place and work. He will
lift this work to a plane where its influence
will radiate new energy to other lives. Love
thinketh no evil. It is the magic atmosphere
through which no evil can pass. In this atmosphere of love, in making haste to be kind,

one becomes a part of all that spiritual potency which surrounds him. Then can he say, " I and my Father are one." Then can he realize his divine nature, which is his true nature, his essential self; then will he dwell on the Mount of Vision.

The struggle toward the more unselfish and loving life is, in itself, success.

"Say not the struggle naught availeth, — "

it avails always.

It avails, too, in shaping and creative power. The effort to keep in touch with all that is highest allies one with the currents of infinite energy. It brings one into a state receptive to the heavenly magnetism. Instead of drifting blindly at the mercy of chance currents, he can intelligently control and shape his purposes.

He shall live, too, in the atmosphere of exhilaration. He shall find the yoke easy and the burden light. He shall be filled with the heavenly magnetism, and life shall grow finer and sweeter day by day.

It is success when one overcomes the thought
of self, or self interest, and loses it in generous
outgoing purpose. It is success when he
substitutes the higher for the lower range of
enjoyments. For then alone is he truly living; only then can he find his soul's native
air, and set his feet in the path that grows
more beautiful day by day.

   *   *   *   *   *

Magnetize the Conditions. "Behold, I make all things new."
This is the message of every New
Year. We live by ideals and enthusiasms and convictions and visions. That
which we see, as in vision; those conditions
in which we habitually picture ourselves in
mental imaginings, — are those which shall
be materialized in outward fact.

Thus the shaping of our lives is entirely
within our own power. The philosophy of
it is possible to comprehend. It is by a law
as inevitable as the law of gravitation. It is
by means of the spiritual power by which we
stamp a mental image upon the plastic material
of the invisible, or the astral conditions. Those

conditions in which one persistently sees himself, in mental vision, he is thereby creating. It is not wrong to wish for power, in whatever guise it may come, — as wealth, or fame, or any form of force and energy. The more power to use the better, — if one but use it aright. "All power is given to Me in heaven and earth," said Jesus. And again He promises that the works which He does we shall do also, and "greater works than these." This is not only a possible privilege, but a responsibility and a duty. It is part of the divine inheritance to grow into this knowledge and power.

And the way is Love. This is the utmost potency, the divine energy. The spiritual conditions of all bloom and brightness and blessedness of life are love and harmony, or that harmony that is the result of love. To be glad in the gladness of others; to rejoice in ministering in every possible way to any need or want; to never fail, as Phillips Brooks said, to bring the largest sympathy to the smallest trouble; to live in that spirit of thoughtful and

generous consideration that we may miss no
least opportunity of service; to meet the need
of the moment if we can, regardless of using
the resources that prudence would lay up for
the future, — this is the spirit which creates
the conditions of power and happiness.

There is the deepest philosophical as well
as ethical significance in that passage in the
Scriptures, "Let the words of my mouth and
the meditations of my heart be alway accept-
able in Thy sight, O Lord, my strength and my
Redeemer." For it is out of thought spoken
and unspoken that are the issues of life. That
which one habitually feels and says is that
which determines his entire life in its external
aspects and its inner states. If one wishes,
then, to build up his fortunes, or his character,
or his achievements, to strengthen and enlarge and exalt all, the place to begin is in his
own mind. When the apostle Paul exhorts to
a new and higher life, what method does he
recommend? "Be ye transformed," he says,
"*by the renewing of your mind.*" And again,
"Let every soul be subject unto the higher

powers." Words could be multiplied to any
extent, repeating and emphasizing this truth in
its twofold aspect, — that life is determined,
in both its quality and its achievement, by the
inner thought, and that the inner thought is
determined by the extent to which it allies
itself with the higher powers.

In this closing decade of the nineteenth
century science as well as ethics has laid hold
of this truth.   No longer is it only an enthusi-
astic expression of religion, but an exact expression of science.   Scholarly research as
well as spiritual activity accepts it, and the
principle is formulated under the name of
psycho-physics.   There has been for some time
past in Washington an eminent savant engaged
in this work of scholarly research into that
mysterious and most intimate connection of
thought and form.   Prof. Elmer Gates has
already attracted great attention by his re-
searches into the very springs of life, which is
described by a scientific writer as follows : —

"Every thought which enters the mind is registered in the brain by a change in the structure of

the cells. The change is a physical change more or less permanent. Bad thoughts build up structures of cells which engender evil ideas, and good thoughts contrariwise. Consider the case of the man who is unhappy and depressed, who has lost ambition and walks the streets with a slouching gait. The psycho-physicist can take such a person and within six weeks transform him to such an extent that every friend of his will notice the difference."

This change is produced simply by magnetizing the mental conditions. Not only can this be accomplished by the psycho-physicist, but by any one for himself, if he but come into a comprehension of the law. Such changes in personal bearing and appearance can be brought about without a word of specific counsel regarding gait or awkward bearing. It will be a natural outward conformation resulting from an inner change. The man will simply be trained to rehearse pleasant memories and to hold agreeable thought for so many hours every day, as the body might be put through certain gymnastic training so many hours a day. Any person may practise it for himself,

and the entire philosophy is condensed in
those words of the apostle, that " Whatsoever
things are pure, lovely, and of good report.—
think on these things."

Regarding this process, Mr. Henry Wood
says: " Every one has long been aware that
fear, grief, sin, anxiety, pessimism, and all their
train pull down bodily tissue ; but we have un-
wittingly failed to observe that their positive
opposites would surely build it up.   But this
is logical and reasonable.   Harmony, joy,
optimism, idealism, love, and courage will
surely invigorate.   Under the now well-under-
stood law of auto-suggestion and thought concentration, each mental condition can be
positively cultivated and made dominant in the
consciousness.   It is possible to entirely change
the mental habit."

This is the method by means of which one
may immediately modify, subsequently change,
and continue to control his life, in all its outward aspects and circumstances.   Determining
a high order of thought registers an exactly corresponding physical change in the brain cells.

Produce good brain cells, and they, in turn, produce good and prosperous thought. It is a matter of action and reaction. Beyond this, one may at any time put his psychical stamp on the day, — determining all its hours to yield sweetness, peace, progress, and love.

Professor Gates asserts, that, in the case of art students who are giving, one may say, eight hours a day to technical study, if they would give two hours of these daily to absolute silence and solitude, to receive and absorb the art impressions and suggestions in the universe, — bring themselves in communication with the infinite storage of art thought which there exists, — they would progress much more rapidly than if devoting the entire time to external activities in drawing, modelling, or painting.

In every specialty of work this same principle holds true. The secret of inspiration lies in the hour of silent spiritual communion with the unseen.

Henry Wood clearly teaches the potency of thought when he says : —

"We should think just as though our thought were visible to all about us. Real character is not outward conduct, but *quality of thinking*. The teaching of the Great Exemplar on this point was positive, but the world has ignored its scientific exactness."

When the higher promptings are disregarded they grow fewer, and perhaps cease altogether. Opportunity is a good angel, but she deserts those who fail to recognize her. The ring of power must be worn, not let fall into the sea. If the charm is not held to service it slips away.

> And he that with a slackened will
>   Dreams of things past, or things to be,
> From him the charm is slipping still,
> And drops, ere he suspects the ill,
>   Into the inexorable sea.

It is not at all necessary to be what the world calls consistent; it *is* necessary to be true. It is necessary to follow the clue thrown to one from the labyrinth; it is essential to recognize the opportunity when it comes, and to have the courage to embrace it.

For well, indeed, does Mrs. Whitney somewhere say that, "It is for life, not so much
even for death, that we should be ready;
ready for God's call, which comes to us in
an hour when we know not, and demands
all the strength we should have attained, to
enable us to rise and meet it." The criticism
of caution is transformed to the congratulation
of courage, whenever that courage has proved
itself a success. And the royal road to success is to obey the inner genius, to act in
accordance with one's own intuitions, regardless of the fear or favor of those who are bound
to the wheel of conventional consistency.

It is little less than marvellous, albeit it is
but the result of a natural law, to discover
the vast extent to which we can reconstruct
external conditions by acting upon them on
the magnetic plane. In Lowell's poem entitled "Longing," these lines occur: —

> "Still, through our paltry stir and strife
>   Glows down the wished Ideal;
> *And Longing moulds in clay what Life*
>   *Carves in the blissful real.*"

Mr. Lowell does not italicize these last two lines, but this form will serve to emphasize here words that must flash upon many of us informed with a new significance. The poet's insight discerned, either consciously or unconsciously, a law that is just beginning to be understood and formulated. The astral world all around us is the clay in which we may model that which events and persons and the tide of influences we have attracted will later carve into the marble of actuality. Before it is carved into this marble of actuality it can be changed, as the artist may change a sketch in clay, or a drawing, before the one becomes sculpture or the other painting. We can experiment, combine, arrange, transform all that is as yet in the astral. It has not yet left our hands. Our higher self may remodel and retouch it. An illustration of this truth, though the circumstance itself is trivial, may possibly make it clearer. Recently a literary worker was detained in an uncomfortable place one night by the accident of missing a train. He was assigned to a room destitute

of the appointments he was accustomed to,
and as the house was near a railroad station
there was noise, and altogether he felt he was
"in for it." The night was damp and muggy,
and the chances for ventilation were very
poor. All this, however, would not have
greatly mattered, only that the next day he
had on hand an important piece of work that
must be entirely complete before night, and
it was not even begun. He wakened about
2 A. M. with a severe headache, greatly aggra-
vated by the noise and the want of air. He
was in despair at the thought of how he should
feel the next day after losing his sleep, — how
illy able to do the quality of writing that his
work required. But he checked himself. He
recalled that the earth is *full* of the goodness
of the Lord; that the entire atmosphere is
magnetic with love and wisdom; that there
are infinite stores, infinite reservoirs of ideas,
of power, of all that his work required. Everything was ready; everything was always
ready; all one had to do was to keep himself
in touch with love and sweetness; in a re-

ceptive condition to the power of illuminating thought.

> " There 's a melody born of melody
> That melts the world into a sea.
> Toil will never compass it," —

he repeated to himself. He asserted, as he
lay there in the darkness, in the close air, the
noise, on an uncomfortable bed and with a
headache, — he asserted his claim to be a part
of the divine universe. " In Him is no darkness." "The Lord is my helper; of whom
shall I be afraid?" "O, send out Thy light
and Thy truth! Let them lead me." He
remembered that there is the divine atmosphere also, as well as the air we breathe, and
that he could draw breath from the Infinite.
In short, he soon fell peacefully asleep, slept
well, and the next morning regained his home.
But now, instead of his work there set in a
series of unforeseen interruptions that could
not be evaded. But he kept his faith. He
kept in the atmosphere of sweetness of spirit,
of receptivity to the heavenly stores. At last

he was released to his task, and he accomplished it in a quarter of the usual time, and produced one of his best efforts. Instead of feeling ill, or less than well, he was conscious of a new tide of energy. Going out that day, he met a friend who gave him certain information especially valuable and encouraging. Nor was it by chance that they met. He had, during his wakeful hour in the night, redeemed the astral conditions from inharmony to harmony. By lifting up his heart to the Lord,.by asserting his oneness with the divine life, he had come under the operation of the higher law. Thenceforth all fell into beautiful order. The conditions were polarized. He was in the relation of receptivity to the Infinite stores.

Now all life is good. "God is light, and in Him is no darkness at all." All life is light, and joy, and gladness, and illumination. And when it seems the reverse to us it is because we have gotten "off the track," as people sometimes say; and the phrase is expressive. We have missed the way. "I am the way," said Christ. If we live in Him and He in us, we do not miss the way.

"Toil could never compass it."

All one's striving could not bring this result; but let him place himself in harmonious receptivity to the Divine power, and he can mould the plastic astral conditions. It is a gift and a grace. It is in this that one finds the secret of

— the untaught strain
That sheds beauty on the rose.

When things go wrong, the magic power to right them is to sit down alone. Go "into the silence." Pray to be taken close into the Divine love. Assert the eternal truth that it is yours, and that you are a part of it. Then will the shadows pass away and the gladness of the Lord shine forth and encompass him round about.

* * * * *

Savoir-Faire. The *savoir-faire* of polite society, although not infrequently the merest veneer, has still its place in the social structure, and the moralist might trace out correspondences, *a la* Swedenborg, on the spiritual side of life. The real quality is always better than the imitation, but even an imitation is not to be despised. The complimentary courtesies are not entitled to any special veneration, if the mere words of pleasant phrasing represent nothing beyond; and still they are the oil to the wheels, the magic that kindles life into something a little brighter. Beyond this, however, is more. One who habitually keeps tone and manner within the limits of entire courtesy feels the reflex influence, and really becomes, more or less — and usually more — that which he seems. It is the *savoir-faire* of the individual which is the saving grace of society. It is not necessarily unselfish, but it simulates unselfishness; and next to loving your neighbor as yourself and therefore giving him some graceful advantage, — next to that is the doing the same thing because it is an attribute of courtesy, a part of good manners. In fact, the perfect charm of good breeding, and the

perfect Christian spirit, must be and are one
and interchangeable and identical, when each
is carried to its ideal possibilities.

There is nothing so beautiful as beautiful
manners. Perfect courtesy is the flower and
fruit of all perfect breeding. It is the one all-
potent and all-determining quality, and when
fulfilled to the utmost it is not far from the
limits of that which is divine.

The power of personality is one whose
potency increases with the finer enlightenment
of modern life. While this charm of personality is to some extent — indeed to a very great
degree — a natural gift, it can also be very
successfully cultivated ; and it is the duty of
every human being to endeavor to cultivate it.
Moroseness and gloom effectually kill out all
the gladness and sunshine of life ; and taking
those away, there is also taken away the
working force, the energy that forms the
motor. In a happy and peaceful frame of
mind all work, or even cares, are comparatively easy to bear ; in moroseness, or bitterness, they are quite the reverse.

It is as easy to cultivate the manner of pleasantness, of ease, of response, as it is to go about in a very atmosphere of the forbidding and repellent. Thought is the one and only force, and it is always possible to think on those things that are pleasant and lovely and of good report. It is largely a habit of mind; and good habits, as well as bad ones, are to a great extent a matter of formation for one's self. Good spirits, as they are called, are half the battle. Any work is half done already if entered upon in a cheerful frame of mind.

An important part in the education of children lies in cultivating the habit of looking on the pleasant side of things rather than the reverse. There is moral efficacy in a joke. Fun and humor are the salt that keeps the savor. To be able to make light of the little ills and accidents of life is to hold the controlling power over them.

There is no experience more disheartening than to encounter the person who, in response to one's casual inquiry as to health and general outlook, responds drearily and gloomily.

Such a disposition makes the encounter with its possessor a burden, — like an avalanche flung on one. It is a serious fault, and one that can and should be overcome. No one has any moral right to go about the world in a state of gloom, carrying with him a bitter, repellent atmosphere. Life is given to be glad in; to use worthily; to make the most of for ourselves and for others. To be pleasant, to be agreeable and responsive and cheerful and uplifting, is an important part of the personal duties of life.

A due self-respect is an integral factor in that serene self-possession which the French so subtly define as *savoir-faire*. A keen illustration of this personal dignity is given by Henry James, in the remark of his hero, Mr. Littlemore (in " The Siege of London "), where that individual is represented as saying: " I hate that phrase, 'getting into society.' One ought to assume that one is in society, that one *is* society, and to hold that if one has good manners one has, from the social point of view, achieved the great thing. The

rest is for others." It is, indeed, quite time
that the popular phrases — a "society girl,"
a "woman of society" — should receive this
delicately implied reproach. As currently
used they are — not to put too fine a point
upon it — simply vulgarisms; because they
are chiefly current among the half-way people,
— the people to whom "society" is synonymous with a vague perspective of balls, dinners, receptions, *et cetera,* and to whom the
cultivation of the heels quite takes precedence of the cultivation of the head. To
define this element of the world as society,
exclusively, is to limit it to its crudest possible
signification. True society has a higher meaning than as merely inclusive of a circle of
people of similar incomes per annum who wine
and dine and receive each other, and pay
similar bills to the florist and the caterer.
This form of social cohesion is not materially
higher or finer than the bonds of affinity between Mrs. Tulliver and Mrs. Pullet, who
were conscious of a singular harmony of taste
in the decoration of their china and the

pattern of their table-linen. Society is a spiritual recognition and attraction. It is chemical rather than mechanical in its cohesion. The forces are from within rather than from without. It is hardly possible to over-estimate the power that lies in dress and address; yet it is in its higher rather than its literal significance that one may venture to affirm this, for the merely conventional luxury of fashion, or the Turveydrop style of etiquette acquired in a ballroom, are hardly to be taken as typical of a power for social influence. Good address is the last, best gift of nature; for it is more largely an endowment rather than an acquirement. To the individual possessing it all doors are open. It is the magic key to social success and to business success, and is not without its weight in determining intellectual recognition. While, like art, it is among the natural gifts, it can also, like any branch of art, be highly cultivated. A clear comprehension of what is miscellaneously designated as good manners is the first step toward attaining this grace. Subjected to any kind

of a quantitative analysis, one discovers that
the primary element in good address is self-
control, or the poise, the ease, that results from
self-control.   Serenity is very good to cultivate
to a degree, that whatever occurs, one is not
altogether thrown off one's balance.   High
tragedy off the stage becomes worse than poor
comedy.   The well-bred woman has a latent
poise that is not too easily disturbed by incident or accident.   In referring to dress as
a social power, it is not intended to imply
rich or extravagant apparel, but, instead, that
which is suitable to the attendant circumstances.   Character must always take precedence of appearance; yet appearance, too, has
its weight.   With the consciousness of being
suitably dressed, one may dismiss all self-
consciousness.   To remember one's self in the
dressing-room, and forget one's self in the
drawing-room, is sensible counsel.   The days
have far receded into the past when to be a
literary woman implied being a woman without taste or conformity to the modes.   Women
who, in any manner, come prominently before

the world recognize it as a duty to themselves
and to all other women to dress as well and
as suitably as possible. General appearance,
dress and address, go in this age for all they
are worth as social powers. One's life is not
determined by what some one else may think
of it. Let that pass.

> "Seek not the spirit if it hold
> Inexorable to thy zeal!"

Well may one ask himself,

> "Am I not, also, real?"

In its best significance *savoir-faire* is the outward sign of inward serenity and convictions of
personal reality.

* * * * * *

**Finance
and
Integrity.**
The career of a capitalist is one
of peculiar fascination to the fem-
inine mind. Not in that strict sense
of the term in which it might be applied to a
Gould or a Vanderbilt, or even to the ordinary
millionaire, but a very humble and rudimentary type of a capitalist, as the woman who
sets up a bank account for herself may be.

The difference between the plus or the
minus hundred dollars may really make to her
all the difference in the world between that exhilaration of spirits born of self-respect and a
consciousness of owing no man anything, or
that vague depression and discouragement
caused by being in debt. Nor does it matter
so greatly whether the balance in the bank, on
the one hand, or the debt due which she cannot pay, on the other hand, be small or large,
so far as peace of mind goes. It is as uncomfortable to owe a hundred dollars which one
cannot pay, as to owe a thousand which he
cannot meet. All these things are relative,
and the small transactions, to a small income, are just as important as are the large
ones to the great income. There is a most
important part of education for women in
gaining a practical and experimental knowledge
of finance. A definite allowance and a check-
book will make of many a woman an econo-
mist and a manager, who otherwise would be
a wasteful spendthrift, — on a small scale,
doubtless, but one quite as extravagant in

relation to her means as are the titled dàmes of high degree in London, who are hopelessly in debt to their milliners and tailors.

There is something in that exactness of figures — those inexorable figures which tra ditionally will not lie — that educates a woman. She resists frivolous temptations. She does not buy frippery that she does n't want because it is on the "bargain counter." She restrains her inclinations for many a tem porary temptation of the moment rather than draw a check and decrease her little store by so much, to pay for it. And in the end she is doubtless better off without it than with it. There is great strength of character gained, sometimes, in doing without. It is surprising to see how soon five dollars saved here and ten there amounts to a hundred, and that is worth leaving intact in the bank.

The use of money is largely a matter of personal character. We spend our money for what we like, and we are like that for which we spend our money. For money is repre-

sentative. It can be drawn upon for mere
self-indulgences of a material character, for
purely decorative purposes, or it can be made
to represent books and art and culture and
travel. It can be economized wisely, so that
one can enjoy the luxury of doing without
something she desires, and helping another
who has a genuine need. The educational
exactness of a bank account fosters all this
self-denial, this discrimination of selection and
moral integrity. For at the last analysis
moral and financial integrity are very closely
identical, and the individual who incurs bills
which he has no reasonable prospect of paying,
is not greatly better than the criminal who
obtains money dishonestly. The integrity of
finance is a very sure test of character.

It is to be regretted that the terms meanness and economy are not infrequently considered as synonymous and interchangeable;
and that the individual who gives a thought
to saving a dime, a quarter, or a dollar, is
thereby considered as less generous, less considerate, than he who spends profusely; yet a

second thought may show that it is thought-
less and lavish expenditure which is selfish,
and a reasonable regard for economy which is
unselfish; that there may be a spending
which is merely idle waste and a saving which
has its object in spending, — in a way to
represent higher needs than the caprice of the
moment.

Take, for example, the fad of the day that it
is more polite in the city to send notes and letters to friends by special messenger rather than
by post. To pay from fifteen to fifty cents for
messenger service would be no great matter
as an occasional or exceptional thing; but
when this is multiplied every day, and perhaps
several times in one day, it becomes during
the season a sum large enough to have pur-
chased a symphony rehearsal ticket for a
friend who could not obtain one; or an in-
valid's chair to meet a need; or to pay a
girl's board in college; or to make some one
happy with gifts of books or subscriptions to
magazines.

Mrs. Lydia Maria Child was eminent for her

4

genuine thoughtfulness, — that saved on the non-essentials to spend for essentials. Her personal economies were untiring and extremely scrupulous; but when contributions were needed for noble purposes, she had always something to give.

There are few people who, whatever their resources, do not all the time see about them needs they would gladly meet were their means commensurate with their desires; and one aid toward giving one's self this privilege is the habit of small savings, which, in the aggregate, amount to a sum that represents something of importance.

There is a refinement in economy that is not experienced in lavish and reckless spending. The individual who is thoughtful, generous, and considerate is not one to throw away money in the ways of self-indulgence. Money is representative.

Shopping is a matter that can be (and should be) almost reduced to a matter of exact science, and it is one whose best lessons are often bought with that extravagant price of experience. Whether the good shopper is born and not made is open to question; but it is certainly true that there are certain general principles of shopping which can be learned, and thus save the beginner a world of trouble and no little expense as well. Perhaps one of the most important of these principles is to learn to beware of the *ignis fatui* of a "bargain" day without being too sceptical of its possible advantages. This is a custom gradually gaining in American cities, and fashioned after the "occasion" of the Bon Marché of Paris. There are unquestionable advantages to be found on these bargain days; but when one buys goods without any very definite use for them, because, indeed, they are so cheap, the "occasion" becomes a delusion and a snare. The woman who comes home with dozens of yards of ribbons for which she has no immediate or definite use, or "remnants" of choice velvet, or brocade, or pieces of lace, bought because some time they may be a convenience, — such a shopper is a blessing to the trade, but quite the reverse to her·

self and her family. Franklin's old motto,
that "nothing is cheap that you do not want,"
is as applicable to-day as it was a century ago.
Styles of material and colors change with the
seasons, and the corner-stone of to-day is the
rejected stone of next year. One safe principle in shopping is to select one first-class
house and always go to it for one's wares.
In this way one gets the benefit of those
countless favors always shown to the regular
customer; one discovers the exact *locale* of
each department, and can go about without
loss of time, and when special bargains are
to be offered the regular customer receives
timely notice of it. While it may occasionally happen that one would save something
on a certain article by looking about at
other houses, yet on the whole the time and
energy wasted would count for far more than
the trifle saved. And in the long run one
makes much the more economical expendi-
tures and receives the most satisfaction by
patronizing one large and first-class establishment.

True economy does not lie in over-much saving. The thrift that fills attics and closets and storerooms with cast-off clothing, dislocated furniture, odds and ends of stuff of all varieties, is not economy at all, but extravagance and waste. The only mission of things in this transitory world is to be of service to people, and the power of rendering service depends on conditions. There is a very wide gulf fixed between this careful and thoughtful attention to details — seeing that nothing is really wasted, but goes where it can be of service to some one — and meanness or niggardness. Lydia Maria Child, who sometimes wrote to her friends on the backs of old envelopes, was never unable nor unwilling to assist those who needed assistance. Emerson said of Alcott, " He was rich because he was always able to help some one poorer than himself." It is a very easy matter for the wealthy woman to subscribe generously on public subscription lists, and costs far less than does often the continued and perpetual thoughtfulness of the poor woman who is unable to ever give anything of special significance at any one time, but who, nevertheless, meets many daily needs of those immediately about her. A woman whose large possessions and generous thoughtfulness seem almost equal, remarked recently that she had not a storeroom in her house; every scrap and object of any kind left over in her household, from clothing to furniture or kitchen utensils, was at once placed where it would do some one good.

The question of money is the question of the day in the average American home, where there are many and various desires and demands, and those desires which are gratified must be selected from those ungratified. It is impossible to do everything one would like to do; to have everything one might care to have, — and so the matter of choice and selection is all-important. There is a great deal in spending money for those things that contribute to the higher progress and economizing on the more material things. The price of a new carpet, for instance, would go far in the

season toward seeing the really good plays,
hearing some of the finest music, and procur-
ing some of the best reading matter.   All
these things make for culture.   They stimulate the imagination, add to mental resources,
and thus make life happier.   They give one
a reserved fund to draw on in dull days, and
redeem time from growing monotonous.   Now
there is very little pleasure to be gotten out
of a carpet or out of superfine upholstery.
A simple matting on the floor and some good
books about, furnish a room far more attrac-
tively than velvet pile and solid mahogany.
And when the things that one has and the
things one must go without are constantly a
matter of choice, the sense of selection must
be held amenable to the higher ideals of
living.

   "If my neighbor's wealth keeps me in a
condition of continual defiance, I am as much
the slave of it as if it kept me in a condition
of continual obsequience," said Phillips Brooks,
in a discourse entitled, "How to be Abased;"
and the words hold suggestion of practical

importance in life. In a social state in which, happily, the aristocracy of genius and of character holds precedence over that of the mere accident of wealth, the association of the rich and the poor is the rule of life. Intelligence and refinement may exist on five thousand as well as on fifty thousand a year; and in social gatherings, in church, and in philanthropic work the comparatively rich and comparatively poor woman must meet daily. Some one has recently propounded the conundrum, "What shall we do with our millionaires?" and one use to make of them was suggested in that they should be permitted, or constrained, to undertake all the costly fitting up of general life; that if a town needed a new hall, or a library, or a court-house, or a fountain, its millionaire shall forthwith fall to and build it, while those who were not millionaires should passively accept and enjoy it. This is an ingenious and truly original solution of the matter; but it is more than an open question if there would be a kindness in making nine-tenths of the community "pauperized by inaction," while the other tenth should provide for their welfare. There is value in the doing as well as in being done for; a blessedness in serving as well as in being served, and one that those poor in worldly goods can by no means afford to miss. The wealth of our neighbors would serve a poor use if it reduced us to inactivity, to envy, or to defiance. If it has this effect it certainly keeps us in a most abject condition of spiritual slavery. On the other hand, the home of wealth may become not only a social centre, but a centre of culture as well; a fountain of hospitality, in a mental and an artistic sense, from which those who enter go away richer than before. It is good to live, one's self, amid beautiful surroundings; but if this cannot be, it is a privilege to go into the home where wealth permits beauty and art, and enjoy it in the fine appreciation of its richness of life. The woman who is envious, or defiant, or in any way disturbed because her neighbor has a more elaborate and luxurious establishment, or greater privileges of life than herself, proves that she is unfitted to enter into higher privileges. Not that the gift is invariably to the most deserving. The race is not always to the swift nor the battle to the strong, but there is one unchanging truth, — that it is far better to appreciate and not to possess, than to possess and not to appreciate.

OUR BEST SOCIETY.

Do we ever call any man good unless we believe that he is interested in the happiness of others ; unless he uses his power and his means for the promotion of their welfare?

To be good, one must be "good for something;" one must fill a place and make an unselfish use of power. Goodness always means good will; and good will always implies relations with other beings.

REV. CHARLES GORDON AMES.

THE ART OF CONVERSATION.

CONVERSATION is so exclusively the expression of life, the unerring register of its quality, that all the world technically known as "society," all human intercourse, — indeed, all occasions of meeting, — are to be judged by the quality of conversation they suggest; and this conversation is the fundamental reason of all this contact. So that the entire social world, with its fêtes and entertainments ; in its apportionment of work or its margin of leisure, its devotion to thought and culture and philanthropy, — all these are the crucible from which is distilled the alembic of conversation.

It is more than an open question if we do not all find untold enjoyment in the caller who comes because she really wishes to see her hostess, — incredible as so old-fashioned a motive may be, — and who is not relieved by

finding that her friend is out. The privilege
of having some one with whom we may exchange a few rational words every day, as
Emerson phrases it, is the choicest gift in life.
We are rich in society and yet poor in companionship. In the overflow of chatter we are
starved for conversation. Social life is so
largely an affair of representation, it inclines
so largely to the spectacular and to what its
chroniclers designate as "social functions,"
that the element of conversational intercourse
is almost eliminated. Yet, primarily, is not
that the supreme object of all friendly meeting? When we reduce to first principles this
complex thing called living, do we not go to
our friend solely to talk with him? Do we
not invite him solely that we may exchange
ideas and compare views on subjects of mutual
interest? Still, as things go, people meet all
through a season in the midst of groups and
throngs — at dinners, receptions, entertainments of all kinds — without exchanging one
word in the way of true intercourse. They
fail to find the clue to the labyrinth of inner

life. They know no more of each other's
tastes and convictions than as if they did not
meet at all. This must always be, so long as
the social ideal is gregarious rather than re-
strictive; so long as it is held to be a waste
of time to give an evening to one friend, alone,
rather than to a dozen, or a hundred. Yet
the delight of the little dinner where conversation in a real sense of interchange of thought
is possible, of the running talk in privileged
intimacy of sympathetic companionship, is far
and beyond any other of the enjoyments possible to human life; and it is singular that those
persons who possess the luxury of commanding
their time should not include this pleasure
among the diversions of their days. In the
multitudinous voices of earth this music of the
spheres is lost.

That the hostess should issue her invitations
from any absolute idea of actually desiring to
meet the person invited is ruled out of modern
considerations. The law of selection rests on
another basis. The hostess is paying her
social debts. She is cancelling her obligations

to those whose entertainments she has graced, and whose ices she has eaten; and the chief concern regarding her own affair is that her guests shall be warmed, lighted, fed, and amused on the same costly scale as that on which they have warmed, lighted, fed, and amused her. The reciprocity treaty, however unknown to our government, prevails largely in society. Certainly it has the advantage of dispensing with many subtle and complex conditions that have sometimes haunted the brain of mankind.

In the diary of Pepys he records, after an evening spent in the great world, " But, ye gods ! what poor stuff it was they did talk ! " The remark must occur to most of us now and then in any critical review of the topics or discussions of the hour where inanities usurp the place of ideas. Conversation is an art, — perhaps the finest of the fine arts, — the one which includes all others as tributary to its perfection. Knowledge and accomplishments are a basis for good conversation ; but without original gifts they do not insure the good talker. Given, abstract learning with culture, — which is only learning assimilated rather than *en bloc*, — with swift sympathies, keen appreciations, and a touch of imaginative power which adds the dramatic element, and there are combined the ideal conditions to make a good conversationalist. The good talker must, of all things, be facile; he must possess the charm of the touch-and-go, — not degenerating into mere flippancy; not losing the instinctive sense of values, but still hold-ing that fluency and flexibility which differ-entiates the interesting man from the bore. For nothing is more trying to the nerves than the man who is forever in saying nothing; whose conversation is of the heavy monologue style; who gives a half-hour's reply to a half minute's question. The Inquisition itself could not furnish torture keener than this.

"I talk," said Dr. Holmes, "not to tell what I think, but to find out what I think." This expresses perfectly the art of conversa-tion. It is experimental. It is an encounter of wits, of commentators on events or ideas;

and it is the means whereby suggestion, insight, and new points of view are obtained. Conversation is direct personal revelation. It should be inspirational in its touches, brilliant in glancing allusion; in the quick change, the current coin of society.

* * * * * *

Entertaining Friends. It is a curious commentary on our civilization that we can find no higher means of expressing our respect or admiration for a friend, or a stranger, than to give a dinner in his honor. Is this the lingering relic of barbarism, of savagery, in our nineteenth — almost twentieth — century civilization? Are we still in such poverty of imagination that we can think of no other way of testifying to our appreciation of a distinguished or an especially beloved individual than to offer him food?

An invitation sent recently from a lady in the suburbs to a friend in town seemed to its recipient to be in its way an ideal of the most refined and advanced type of courtesy. It was to the effect of — "Come out — such and

such a day. Take any train that suits your
convenience. Do not try to avoid meal-time.
If you are hungry I will feed you, after the
Bible injunction." Now this was putting
things in their true relation. It was the visit,
the conversational intercourse, the communion
of spirit that this hostess offered. She paid
her invited guest the very rare and delicate
compliment of assuming that a lunch or a
dinner *per se* was no inducement to go out of
town for a day. If she wanted lunches or
dinners they abound in every hotel or restaurant. But conversational interchange, — the
range of discussion, of comparison, of sympathetic comprehension and imaginative grasp, —
ah, these do not abound in restaurant or hotel.
They are not to be bought with a price.
They are the gift of friendship only; and it
was to this supremest of gifts and grace that
the hostess had bidden her friend. "Come to
me as you will. We will meet and sympa-
thize and re-inspire each other." That was
the essence of it. Is there not something
finer in this than the mere material, stupid

formality, " Will you dine with me at seven ? "
— the dinner being put forward as the essential, and the conversation left as an unimportant and accidental detail.

There are those who say that dinner-giving
is a fine art.   The caterer regards exact knowledge as to the relative merits of clear or thick
soups, and the composition of sauces, with
reverence similar to that of the astronomer for
exact knowledge of the stars in their courses.
But are we, the heirs of all the ages, to accept
this as an intellectual standard?   It is true
that the high-art dinner, so to speak, with its
decorations, its beauty of service, and its general decorum, is an elaborate social function,
but at its best conversational opportunities
are far less than the drawing-room can offer.
The presence of servants, the changes of
courses, the fixed positions, are all far less
favorable to social interchange than where
people can group as they please in library or
drawing-room ; and to make the giving of a
ceremonious dinner the highest form of our
testimonial argues that we are still far removed

from the finer appreciation of the higher values
of life.

"Society," says Kate Field, "ought to be
the best expression of humanity; one of these
days it will be."

In this terse and true assertion Miss Field
touches, as she is apt to do, the very key-
note of life. A leader, and one who has,
indeed, taken the initiative in some of the
more important reforms among the social
problems of the day: working from a logical
basis, she is yet always the idealist who sees
truth in its larger aspects and its more delicate
scale of values. However false or frivolous
or trite or trivial society may be in existing
phases, she looks beyond when regarding it,
and portrays it in the ideal state, which is the
permanent reality. Society is, after all, but
the aggregation of individual relations, — of
loves and friendships and acquaintanceships;
and the more ideal the individual the more
ideal is society. The basis of its ideal state is
love. The ecstasy of life is in doing something
for others, — not for one's self. Narrow and

monotonous is the life centred in its own interests. It is redeemed to high uses, to noble outlook, to thrilling joy only by entering into the widest possible range of sympathies and vivid appreciations.

We live by our enthusiasms and our exaltations. Our sympathies are our strength. Our interests are our magnetisms, and are transmuted into our working capital. It is good for one to have some strong and sudden need arouse all his latent energy and lead him to test his resources by measuring them against the demand. Society will come more clearly into the realization as well as the recognition that service is the supreme luxury of existence. "He that is greatest among you, let him be your servant." He that has the greater joy is he who may minister, rather than he who is ministered unto. It is he who accepts the service and the ministry who confers the reward.

Aristocracy is a very real and fine thing, — so real that it is to be had in no vulgar market-place. But it consists in a mental attitude, — not in material possessions and accumulations.

To see the mere plodding grabbers of pelf pose as social aristocrats is inimitably ludicrous, — the people whose lives are given over to greed and gain, and who are so dull as to imagine that a full purse conceals poverty of spirit. There is nothing inherently vulgar in trade and traffic, in business and commerce. It is quite possible to find a great and beautiful and lofty nature in business, and a very petty one in the haunt of the scholar or the artist; but when greed and getting and gain own the man, rather than are owned by him and reduced to ways and means of reasonable service, then is he on dangerous ground. The true aristocrat measures humanity by finer standards than those of visible accumulations. He could not descend to so plebeian and paltry a thing as selfishness or greed. *Noblesse oblige.* To be courteous to one's peers is all very well, but it is fairness and courtesy and consideration to those in dependent or limited conditions that constitutes the true test of the gentleman or the lady. It is in this that the inherent aristocracy of good family and good

breeding is revealed. True aristocracy is not
at all a matter of possessions, but of quality of
spirit. Its range will never be found by the
statistics of the income tax. It is written in
another language. When the street-car conductor with gentle courtesy raises a woman's
umbrella, holding it over her as she steps
off in the rain; or when the boor, though
he be a multi-millionaire, rudely bars the way
and allows people to pass as best they can
with no consideration from him, — who is the
gentleman? who is the true aristocrat? When
the hostess selects her guests on the basis of
those who can entertain sumptuously in return,
or on the basis of agreeable social qualities, —
which is the more truly aristocratic? There is
no aristocracy in merely a group of rich people
with vulgar ideas, and among whom ideals are
conspicuous by their absence. Wealth and
aristocracy not infrequently go hand in hand,
because there is refinement, courtesy, and love,
and the larger resources of wealth simply
offer added means for the carrying out of noble
purposes; but always is it true that aristo-

cracy in any true sense is a personal quality,
and not at all a matter of family or of possessions. It is an attribute whose manifestations are integrity, courtesy, and honor. The
true aristocrat is not afraid of appearing
in the most simple and inexpensive garb,
but he is afraid of going in debt. He is not
ashamed to work, to economize, to do any
honest and useful thing. Being born royal,
he dignifies whatever he undertakes. It must
be a very poor sort of person who regards
his sole claim to social consideration to lie
in the cut of his garment or the locality of
his house.

"The best expression of humanity." This,
indeed, is what society should be, and, as Miss
Field so truly says, "one of these days it will
be." A deeper spirituality will do away with the
pettiness of strife and greed. More truly will
we realize that the earth is full of the riches of
the Lord, and that each may have all that his
thought, his spiritual attitude, draws to him.
A high purpose is magnetic and attracts rich
resources. One need not be anxious or wor-

ried. " For your Father knoweth what things ye have need of before ye ask." These are not idle words nor empty promises. They are as real, as practical, as the laws of income and outgo. One's resources are merely the manna of the day, to be drawn upon and used, — not hoarded; there is an abundance for to-morrow. " The earth is *full* of the riches of the Lord," and one may give himself the luxury of supplying the need he sees, of meeting the want, glad and grateful that he be permitted the joy of service, without any weak and ignoble cavilling about its effect on his future prosperity or present resources. If he obeys the divine law he is in the current of progress. When this great truth is realized and lived every day by each and all, then will society be the best expression of humanity.

" The ornaments of a home are," indeed, " the guests who frequent it."

Entertaining is the finest of all the fine arts, and it cannot be done by proxy. It cannot be done by the cook nor yet by the decorator.

The hostess cannot order it from the florist, nor the caterer, nor the professional "performer," — whether of music or Delsarte recitals. To depend upon these shows a poverty of resources. And more than all, and above all, every entertainment, whether informal or ceremonial, may well be based on the spirit of those words: " Better a dinner of herbs where love is than a stalled ox and hatred therewith." Let the hostess give her guests her personal interest, her warm friendship, her sympathetic comprehension, and she will have then mastered the delicate and subtle art of entertaining.

The advent of guests in the home should be, ideally speaking, a delight, and not a drudgery. It might always be so rather than to assume the proportions of a domestic problem, if the hostess would realize that it is her welcome that charms her guest and not a display beyond the usual line of her living.

Let us not entertain too visibly, too tangibly, but share with the guest our usual daily life rather than manufacture for him an arti-

ficial life. He will perceive the sham and
will not enjoy it.

When informal entertaining can be established purely on the basis of social meeting
and greeting, and the pleasure anticipated be
that of conversational intercourse, society will
be a finer and higher thing than it is to-day.
If, to invite fifty or one hundred friends for the
informal four-to-six, the hostess must look to the
florist, the caterer, and professional or amateur
musicians or readers, in order to entertain her
guests, obviously her entertainments must be
restricted in number unless she is the possessor
of unlimited wealth. But if she herself is
accomplished in that finest of fine arts, entertaining : if she knows how to bring people
together ; how to group them as skilfully as
flowers in a bouquet ; how to evolve the
harmonies of each nature ; how to suggest,
stimulate, inspire, — then she may well be
freed from any tyranny and dread of expenses
she can illy afford, and of results that are
more or less commonplace even after they are
achieved.

The responsibility of the hostess is far less
for the "warming, lighting, and feeding" her
guests than it is for the personal happiness of
every one who crosses her threshold. A woman
may refrain from inviting as she pleases; but
having once bidden any person beneath her
roof, she becomes responsible for his (or her)
happiness while there. This is the law and
the prophets. It is simply amazing to see
the utter indifference sometimes with which a
hostess will invite some one who is a stranger
to all the rest of her guests, and precipitate
this stranger into a room full of people, all of
whom are more or less familiar with each
other, and leave him to his fate. It is the
business of the hostess to introduce some one,
at least, of her more familiar friends to the
stranger; some one who will present others,
and draw him within the current, and make
him feel at home. If she has not sufficient
tact and forethought and kindliness to do this,
she lacks the essential gifts and grace of the
hostess.

*   *   *   *   *

The Charm of Atmosphere.   The supreme ideal of a home, as of an individual, is that of charm; and to invest one's belongings with this charm of atmosphere is to offer the saving grace to social life.

The interesting person is never *mal à propos.* He can never interrupt, no matter how busy you are; for he supplements and vivifies rather than breaks the thread of thought. He can never come too often nor stay too long. The quality of interest is due to no single gift, grace, or acquirement that can be specified; it is rather a flavor, an essence, an atmosphere. It is as incapable of definition as is any form of enchantment.

The social lion may serve for a jest and witticism at pleasure; but the social star is a different affair. Society is as subtle in its attractions and repulsions as is a chemical compound. Elective affinities determine its composition. The entrance of a stranger into any special coterie where mutual intimacy prevails is at once productive of changes in one way or another, serving to separate or

unite others into closer, or into different, relations. This fact indicates the responsibility
inherent in all social intercourse. For people
to suppose they must find their religion, in
the sense of spirituality, at church, and their
frivolity at a dinner or a reception, is to take
a narrow and an unworthy view of human
life. Spirituality, exaltation of purpose, are
everywhere communicable; and it is not only
the privilege of the hour, but its higher duty,
to communicate such purposes. This is not to
say that one should go about with tracts and
with gratuitous advice to bore people to death
and disenchant them with the very thought of
earnestness or exaltation. It is character, not
exhortation, that truly influences. The most
potent influence is the unanalyzed; that which
is felt, not formulated. "The presence of a
noble nature changes the lights for us," says
George Eliot. "We feel that we, too, can be
seen and judged in the wholeness of our conduct." To come in contact with this noble
nature at a lunch, a tea, may be as valuable as
to attend a church service, or a lecture. It is

uplift of spirit that is everywhere communicable, and it is the simple duty of every well-bred person to hold himself amenable to this social responsibility.

What more underbred and philistine thing can there be than the woman who seizes the occasion of a social meeting to give some unpleasant thrust? — and still one meets this in what is supposed to be good society. Should not the term be restricted to the society of good people?

Good conversation is the prime factor in the atmosphere of charm. It is the tragedy of life when people have nothing to say that is worth the saying or the hearing. They have read the latest novel; they have heard the last opera; they have met the reigning social lion. But what have they to show for it? They will inform you that they like — or dislike, as may be — the novel, the opera, or the individual. And what does that signify? Their personal preferences or prejudices are of no possible consequence. But the woman who can dramatize her im-

pressions, — who has certain definite reasons
for the faith that is in her, who can tell
you what the author means in the novel, or
to what degree the artist realizes lyric art,
or who can define for you something in the
personality of the reigning social lion of the
moment, — how rare and how precious does
such a one make the hour! She brings to
life new insights, new magnetisms, new forces.
Conversation is, too, very largely a spiritual
relation. "With one man," says Emerson,
"I walk among the stars, while another pins
me to the wall." Conversation is stimulated,
drawn out, or repressed and extinguished to
a great degree by these mutual magnetisms
of temperament.

It is said that a London belle was asked
to define the gifts and graces that enable a
woman to be a success in society, and that
she laid a special emphasis on a lack of earnestness. There is both truth and sophistry
in this. Earnestness may be a boon or a
bore in social gatherings. All depends. But
earnestness in its better significance is mag-

6

netism and charm. It is the radiating force.
It is the communicative flow of thought and
interchange. It is the one element that lends
charm and purpose to conversation. But it
is a virtue entirely dependent on degree and
direction. It is certainly bad form, if nothing
worse, to be unduly earnest over trifles. It
is bad taste to let earnestness degenerate into
persistence. It is bad taste to grow so earnest over relating some personal experience or
anecdote that the hearer is held an unwilling
prisoner. Better, surely, any form of the
lightness of the fashionable belle rather than
the woman who has a purpose in view, and
persists in keeping it so by her unintermitting
earnestness. But the woman who has sufficient earnestness for ballast, who really has
things to say of actual value, and says them
with a due regard for the limits of time and
the attention due to all, in a social gather-
ing, is certainly far more of a success in
society than she who skims the surface of
superficial affairs. Conversation should be
regarded as an art, and should be sus-

tained with due sense of artistic values in its proportion.

*　　*　　*　　*　　*

The Modern Corinna. When the announcement was made that the University of Heidelberg was about to admit women to the Philosophical Faculty and give to them its degree, it was recognized as one whose interest and importance far transcended that of its specific measure, important as was that alone ; for it is one of the signs of the times which hold a special significance. Heidelberg recently celebrated its 500th anniversary, and its great age and the conservative German spirit are two factors in the case which would not have been regarded as favorable to so radical and progressive a movement. If, then, the ancient university of which least would have been expected in the way of liberal ideas regarding the higher education of women opens its doors to them, how encouraging is the outlook ! If this concession prove satisfactory at Heidelberg, all departments of the venerable institution will then be opened to women.

Few countries have held more conservative ideas regarding woman's place in the social economy than Germany. Of late years several German women have worked with great energy for the diffusion of truer views. Among these, notably, is Fräulein Helene Lange. The influence of the Empress Frederick has always been thrown on the side of progress. Public sentiment is surely, though slowly, becoming enlightened, but it has its way to make against the inherited prejudice of ages.

But the leaven of the truer conception of women's possibilities is working everywhere, — in Japan, in Germany, in England, and in our own country. There is accumulating an immense reserved force of silent thought which will burst into bloom, which will externalize in action in a way that will seem strangely sudden to those unacquainted with this long preliminary preparation. All great events at last come with swift and sudden power, although the causes may have been long in operation.

It is now only some thirty-five years since Vassar College, the first provision made for

the higher education for women in this
country, was opened; but to-day we see
in prosperous working Smith, Bryn Mawr,
Wellesley, Radcliffe, with co-education at Cor-
nell, Boston University, the University of
Michigan, and many others, and Yale's first
initial movement toward opening her doors
to women.

It is the opening of the great universities
to women on equal terms with men that is
now the great desiderata in education. No
new college can give the spirit, the association, the thrill of life that has been commu-
nicated by generations of scholars, as can
the established universities. The women's
colleges are better than no college at all,
but they are a meagre and imperfect substitute for the advantages offered in an older
university; and not until their entire resources
are open to women on equal terms with men
will the ideal of the higher education of
women be attained.

Now and then one sees some expression
in the newspapers to the effect of embody-

ing a general supposition that if a woman
be eminent for education or special gifts or
acquirements, it is regretted that she does
not extend her life beyond her home. It
suggests an inquiry into the relative virtues
of public and private living. Is it the life
outside the home that demands, exclusively,
the higher virtues? Rather, it is nearer the
truth to believe that no life requires so complete and harmonious a development as that
which holds in its keeping the delicate and
complicated life of home and society. The
woman whose mind has been disciplined by
university study, enriched by classical study,
cultivated by art and literature; the woman
who has had the strength of all these, will yet
find herself taxed by the demands of the home
and social life. All fine threads she holds in
her hands, — not only the ordering of the home,
but, what is far more, the giving of sustaining sympathetic companionship; the hospitality, not only in material sign, but in the
true hospitality of thought, and the sweetness
of spirit that thinketh no evil. The living

force in the community that the ideal woman of private life may be, is a power that exceeds calculation. It is a strength that takes its place among the spiritual forces, which increase and influence in a ratio quite exceeding our human calculations. The most potent force is that of unconscious influence; and the woman who makes her home the centre from which radiates all that is invigorating and uplifting contributes the best possible aid to social progress. To suppose a woman does not require the higher education because she will probably marry, is to put the life of the home, the family, the community as of less importance than the pursuit of some art, profession, or industry. Specific labor may require certain high abilities and definite attainments; but the complicated work that has to do with life itself, in its shaping and formative influences, is the finest of arts and the noblest of professions.

The future of the home is a matter of some concern to the social reformers. But the finer the development and accomplishments

of women through the higher culture into
which they are entering, the more truly will
its benefit elevate and ennoble the home life.

Any plea for the happiness of the home
life — for home life as an end and aim in
itself — does not necessarily imply a plea for
domestic labor on the part of the mistress of
the home. If there is anything that is more
absurd than another in current comment upon
woman's place, it is the praise bestowed upon
the college woman who can cook or who makes
her own gowns. There is no more reason why
the wife should make the bread than there is
that the husband should sweep the sidewalk.
There is no more reason why a woman should
make her own gowns than there is for a man
to make his own coat. And this truth does
not apply exclusively to women of art or professions. Life itself is an art, — the finest of
arts; it is a profession to be at the head of a
home, to superintend its harmonious workings,
to give sweet and sympathetic companionship
in daily household intercourse, and to be always ready to entertain the chance caller or

the invited guest, and not be submerged in
drudgery and detail to the point of excluding
every unforeseen pleasure or privilege that is
offered. It is the unexpected for which one
should always, so far as possible, be ready;
and it is this which not unfrequently lends
the fairest grace to life. The mistress of the
house who allows herself to be imprisoned
under the avalanche of things misses all the
outlook that vision would insure. There is
no intrinsic dignity, honor, or happiness in
broiling a beefsteak or washing the china,
and it is all nonsense to talk about it. As
well require of the merchant at the head of
a great mercantile house that he sweep his
own floor and dust his own counters, or of
the author that he shall go and set up the
type for his own book, or of the president of
a railroad that he perform the duties of brake-
man or porter, as to require of the mistress of a
household that she should personally cook the
food or scrub the floors.

The truth is that housekeeping and home-
keeping have gotten sadly mixed up and mis-

taken,— one for the other.   The finest and
most liberal culture is none too fine to fit a
woman for *home*-keeping; but mere industry
and trained intelligence is the basis of *house*-
keeping.   The woman unlearned in art, literary or social culture, may be a most admirable
house-keeper: it requires intelligence, but it
does not necessarily require culture, to perform domestic service; but the highest and
greatest gifts and the most exquisite cultivation are none too much for *home*-keeping.   It
is a profession of itself more exacting, because
requiring infinitely higher and more varied
resources, than that of the law, of medicine,
of teaching, or of any phase of professional
life.   Its demands are comprehensive, and not
only include the intellectual, but even more
largely all that we call spiritual in its nature,
— of swift recognition, intuitive understanding, and liberal sympathics.   To keep the living coal on the domestic altar is an angelic
and a divine life in its truest and broadest significance; and a popular belief that the more
educated and cultivated is the woman, the

more she must betake herself to professions outside the home, is a signal fallacy. Where is there a position that may be made so influential for good, so capable of rendering constant service to humanity? And it is a fallacy that results from mistaking *house*-keeping for *home*-keeping.

"She was occupied with great themes," wrote Frances E. Willard of her mother after the death of Madam Willard, and the words hold significance. Herein lay the secret — one might almost say the one secret — of a noble, a beneficent life; one in whom met the harmony of spirit and of purpose; whose quality of life was pure, uplifting, and full of stimulus. Health of mind and health of body are the natural results of keeping in such a mental atmosphere as this; health not merely in the negative sense of being free from illness or disease, but in the positive abounding sense of harmony, exhilaration, and purpose. The quality of mental life almost determines that of the physical. The woman whose mind is occupied with great themes has no room in it for petty and corrosive ill temper, or anxieties, or jealousies, or bitterness. And it is the dark and unlovely mental states that produce nine-tenths of the illness and disease of humanity. The physician who will cure will be a metaphysician; one who will realize the higher truth, that physical states and forces are controlled by mental conditions and by the quality of spiritual life.

The value and invigoration of the influence which must go forth from the life of the woman whose mind is " constantly occupied with great themes " is incalculable. And this highly spiritual state represents a duty as well as a privilege. It is the responsibility of each one to so live that he may communicate the better influences, and inspire constantly nobler and finer mental states in all with whom he comes in contact.

To keep in touch with the world of books is one way of being occupied with great themes.

" I joyfully hailed the sight of your handwriting; more joyful even than usual, because

I conjectured that you would write about the biography of Theodore Parker. It is an inspiring book, making one feel that there is nobleness in the battle of life when a true man girds on his armor for the fight. This record confirms my impression that Theodore Parker was the greatest man, morally and intellectually, that our country has ever produced." So wrote Mrs. Lydia Maria Child to a friend; and the lines suggest the helpful inspiration that may lie in noble reading to attune to its own key the level of the daily household life, to sweeten toil and lighten all material burdens.

Instead of the life of the housekeeper, the homekeeper, narrowing itself, and shutting out all intellectual refreshment, it is the life of all others that must needs have that invigoration. It must rise high enough to gain an outlook.

The admirable life of the modern Corinna, who is identified with the professional or the industrial world, is also a notable feature of the social evolution. The qualities that win esteem in the drawing-room win esteem in the counting-room. In the world of affairs, as in the world of home and society, there is no success worthy the name for the woman who is not a lady, and there is no more excuse for her not being a lady in any contact with the world of affairs than there is for her failing to be one in social life. In fact, the refinement, the courtesy, the good breeding, the sweetness of spirit that make a woman esteemed socially are indispensable to her success and to her winning and holding the esteem of her associates, or of those with whom she may come in contact, in the activities of life.

In the increasing avenues of industrial labor opened to women and pre-empted by them, there is not one in which refinement, delicacy, and courtesy will not prevail over self-assertion, aggressiveness, selfishness, or rudeness. It is the gift and grace of womanhood that she may win. Why, then, should she renounce this higher and finer prerogative to descend into strife and demands? She may win a thousand things where she could not command, merely by force, even one. If she could, what then? Are contention and self-assertion qualities to be held as either ideals or necessities in active life? The truth is, indeed, that any woman in industrial, in business, or in professional life, any woman in touch with affairs and activities, needs of all others to *be a lady*, in the highest and sweetest sense that the words imply. Petulance, arrogance, ill temper may be overlooked in the privacy of the home or of the social circle. It will be less easily condoned in the relations of active life.

Dr. Holmes expresses the profoundest truth when he says : —

"It is a woman's business to please. I don't say it is *not* her business to vote, but it is essentially her business to please, and there must be something about her that makes you glad to have her come near."

Nor should it ever be forgotten that sweetness is strength, not weakness. Sweetness of spirit is the inevitable result of spirituality of life. Petulance and ill temper and aggressive qualities are as weak and ineffectual as they are unlovely. Strength is sweetness, and sweetness is strength ; and only out of harmony can success be wrought.

TO CLASP ETERNAL BEAUTY.

For love to clasp Eternal Beauty close,
  For glory to be Lord of self, for pleasure
To live beyond the gods; for countless wealth
  To lay up lasting treasure

Of perfect service rendered, duties done
  In charity, soft speech and stainless days:
These riches shall not fade away in life,
  Nor any death dispraise. — SIR EDWIN ARNOLD

  " By love behold the sun at night."

Love
Asks naught his brother cannot give;
Asks nothing, but does all receive.
Love calls not to his aid events:
He to his wants can well suffice;
Asks not of others soft consents,
Nor kind occasions without eyes,
Nor plots to ope a bolt or gate,
Nor heeds Condition's iron walls, —
Where he goes, goes before him Fate,
Whom he uniteth God installs.
Instant and perfect his access
To the dear object of his thought,
Though foes and land and seas between
Himself and his love intervene. — EMERSON.

7

THE TRUE REALITIES.

HE most real thing is one's own soul. That may be set down as an axiom; and being true, the real business of life is to keep one's soul in the state of harmony, of love, of joy, in which alone is the condition of creative activity. As the most real thing is the soul, so the most unreal thing is any quality opposed to spiritual states, — as envy, hatred, or despair. The circumstances or events that throw us into any of these conditions render us negative to true advancement. And so, measuring life by the ideal, one has no moral right to let himself be so disappointed or depressed or disturbed as to be in any wise turned aside from his real business, — the right living.

Still, in that all of us are more or less fallible human beings, we often fall into grievances. The wrong things happen, or the right

thing happens at the wrong time. The thing
we expected eludes us; events go awry;
friends disappoint us, and we meditate over
the numerous delightful things they could do
for us just as well as not, and that they fail to
do. We conclude it is a cold and unfeeling
world, and set ourselves to the key of being
quite as cold and unfeeling as any one else
can be. All of which is not only quite un-
heroic, but extremely ridiculous. If a man
finds, or thinks that he finds, that no one
loves or respects him, then let him by all
means love and respect himself; not with
egotism and absurd self-love, but with that
kind of self-respect that recognizes that his
life is his responsibility, that he is in the
world primarily for development, and that if
his next-door neighbor does not care for him,
it is not a matter of supreme importance.
For he is living for himself; for purposes
and duties of his own, and not for the
approval or admiration of other people, —
pleasant and grateful as that may be. It is
something always most precious to receive;

but it is always possible to live, and live worthily, without it. For one's life is, primarily, between himself and the Lord, and not between himself and human relations, although it is through those relations and by means of them that he must, for the most part, live his human life. But the mainspring of any life worth the living is its own divine Ideal, which quickens and informs it. It is not a mere phrase of words to say that life must be lived "as unto the Lord." This embodies the entire philosophy, the one true ideal of its conduct.

The most real thing in a man is his soul. No misunderstanding, no undervaluing of other people, can take that away from him. If they regard him as ignoble, the best reply is simply to be noble. Their belief need not create his own reality. If they believe him selfish, he can reply in generosity; if they believe him disagreeable, he can reply in a life of the utmost courtesy and love. One need not fret himself about misinterpretations. All his concern is simply to live nobly and let other people's impressions take care of themselves. All his concern lies in the being, and not in the seeming. It is one's character, not his reputation, that is of moment. In the end, if not in the beginning, character makes its own reputation ; but to manipulate a reputation does not create a character. One's concern lies in the reality of his own soul.

The chief concern, says some one, is not to be loved, but to be lovely. Therein is condensed the entire truth. And, speaking of love, how remarkably was its infinite and resistless potency brought out in that exquisite little story by Mr. Howells entitled "A Circle in Water." A defaulter and embezzler returns to his family and friends after twelve years in prison. The friends question as to whether the daughter whom he left as a child, and who has been kept in ignorance of this misery, should now be allowed to see her father and learn his sad story. Others speculate as to what the effect of it would be on the potential lover of the young girl. The problem is solved. The lover, when, years after, he ap-

pears, "is apparently sorry" that the poor
father "had not committed worse sins that
he might forgive them for her sake." At all
events they are married, and go to live abroad,
where the father follows them. Mr. Howells
thus ends his story : —

"So far now as human vision can perceive, the
trouble he made, the evil he did, is really at an
end. Love, which can alone arrest the consequences of wrong, had ended it, and in certain
luminous moments it seemed to us that we had
glimpsed in our witness of this experience an infinite compassion encompassing our whole being
like a sea, where every trouble of our sins and
sorrows must cease at last like a circle in the
water."

Love is that all-potent force which can thus
not only create but also dispel conditions.
Love is the reality of the soul. Sufficient
love casts out all evil. The only reply to
hatred is love ; the reply of discord is a
higher harmony, that sweeps everything into
itself.

A most practical application of this truth is

to make it a rule in one's life never to pass on
and communicate fret and jar. If A receive
from B word or note that is annoying, let it
rest there; let him not pass it on to C by tell-
ing him how unreasonable and annoying B is.
Very likely by the time he has repeated it B
is heartily sorry and ashamed of his misdoings,
and would gladly correct them. Then let
love help him to do so. Let love, which can
alone arrest the consequences of wrong, end
it. So shall all life become beautiful and
blessed.

*   *   *   *   *

Another of the Real Forces is Thought. For the real forces of life are in
concentration. "Renounce thine
own will," says one of the mystics,
"and let the law of God only be within thee."
To him, however, who seeks to follow the
law of God, a fallacy sometimes arises like a
spiritual mirage. It lies in the traditional
impression that there is an inherent antagonism between enjoyment and renunciation, and
that, in some undefined way, sacrifice is always
right, and acceptance of privileges is always

wrong. The very fact that a given path is hard and unattractive induces the seeker after the higher life to choose it rather than one which charms him. Now a given matter is not necessarily good because it is hard, or bad because it is easy. The divine leading may be toward Belgravia as well as toward Whitechapel. The rich need ministry as much as the poor, and to deny this is to place a false value on material things. One's true work may lead him amid scenes of beauty as well as in dreary ways. It depends. There are occasions when it is the highest duty to choose hardship and trial, but not because hardship is an end in itself, but an appointed means. Sometimes the same divinely appointed means leads to bloom and beauty instead, and duty does not lose its divineness when it becomes delight instead of drudgery.

Not unfrequently is one's dream his true reality. A youth dreams of art and finds toward it his strongest attraction; but no, he says, in that way lies indulgence, and indulgence is selfish. I will choose the harder

thing. So he renounces his vision, and enters
on the study of law principally because he
does not wish to enter it. The result is a
distorted life. His dream was his reality.
The glory and the sacredness of life is in
developing its finer inclinations. In the development of inclination into impassioned purpose is found its nobler significance. "For
this cause was I born," said Jesus, the Christ,
in reference to his consecrated service. "For
this cause came I into the world." No life
reaches its higher possibilities until it, too, can
say: "For this cause came I into the world."

The time will come when life shall be so
fine a thing that each and every one, everywhere, and always, will live the diviner life
of response and sympathy and social service
in the natural and incidental relations of daily
life. As Prof. Herron says, "Every human occupation should be a communion with God."
If one may but guide his life perpetually by
the law of God, his most casual presence shall
be a gift and a benediction. And what is
the law of God? It is the radiation of love,

sweetness, and exaltation. Into this atmosphere doubt cannot enter. The divine potency within works its way with outward
circumstances, and events fall into the divine
order. To be polarized with the heavenly
magnetism — this it is to realize in daily life
the true realities.

"And, friend, when does thee think?" This
was the question of the Quaker sage to the
youth who was glibly recounting his rush of
amusements and his gay and glittering life,
— "When does thee think?"

The question must recur to all of us in the
electric round of city life, where engagements
press and crowd and throng upon us as we go,
almost breathlessly, from one to another, with
little margin between. There is, of course,
much that one cannot afford to miss: the
opera, the lecture, the dinner-party; the occasion, whatever it may be, that occurs only at
this precise juncture in one's life, and which
must be enjoyed at that hour or not at all.
And we fall into a way of imagining that
thinking is a form of mental activity which

may come any time; which may safely be
relegated to any odd moments not otherwise
filled.   This is not true.   Thought is as
essential to life as is food, — perhaps even
more essential.   For life is not merely, or
even mostly, a matter of physical vitality, but
it must mean intellectual strength and moral
purpose as well.   The poise and exhilaration
and energy, which alone make up any true
living, are the result only of thought and
reflection.   Thought is health; thought is
achievement; thought is success.   It is that
intense psychic potency that can transform
conditions and create new ones.   There is
absolutely nothing in life that cannot be
accomplished by thought.   This is creating on
the ideal plane; and the materialization of it
on the physical plane after its ideal creation
is a mere detail.   Thought is the preparative
process by means of which one comes to be
able to take advantage of opportunity.

To demand for all humanity the equalization of opportunity is an important step in
progress; but to brew some potion that should

insure each and every one to be equal to his
opportunities would be to revolutionize the
world. Indeed, if a man could have one
supreme prayer granted him it might well take
the form of asking that he should always be
equal to his opportunities. The thoughtful
student of life cannot but realize that the
inequalities of fortune lie far less in the range
of opportunities offered than in the capacity
to seize and take advantage of them. As
for success, life is full and overflowing with
chances for success, — chances enough and to
spare for every one. The failure is in the lack
of insight to perceive them, and the swift
power to take advantage of the opportunity as
it presents itself. "It is for life rather than
even death that we should be ready," says
Mrs. Whitney, — "ready for God's call, which
comes to us in an hour we think not, and
demands all the strength we should have
grown to in order to meet it."

Opportunity is the open door. If one has
all his affairs in order and his achievements in
right degree to take advantage of opportunity,

he enters and proceeds on his appointed onward and upward way; if he is unready he
cannot enter. But let him not blame fate for
that. There is always the open door; it is
the vision to perceive it, the capacity to take
advantage of it, that is lacking. To him who
has the vision the delicate omen is traced in
air. And always is it true that —

> "the foresight that awaits
> Is the same genius that creates."

One need not, then, rail and hurl invective
against ill fortune. That is merely the negative
side of good fortune. The ill can be transmuted into good. There is a magic potion, all-
conquering as the potion drank by Tristan and
Isolde, which shall always work the miracle
of success. This magic potion is faith. To
hold one's faith in that supreme degree that it
produces conviction and will, is to hold command over all conditions and situations.
" Prayer is all action," says Balzac, " but it is
spiritual action, stripped of substantiality, and
reduced, like the motion of the worlds, to an

invisible, pure force. It penetrates everywhere, like light; it gives vitality to souls that come beneath its rays, as Nature beneath the sun." Complaint and fret and depression are evil states that annul and paralyze all high action. They are the impenetrable wall through which high thought and pure purposes cannot pass. "To murmur is to forfeit all."

To hold one's self in readiness for opportunity, to keep the serene, confident, hopeful, and joyful energy of mind, is to magnetize it, and draw privileges and power toward one. The concern is not as to whether opportunity will present itself, but as to whether one will be ready for the opportunity. It comes not to doubt and denial and disbelief. It comes to sunny expectation, eager purpose, and to noble and generous aspiration.

*   *   *   *   *

Be Swift to Love. The preacher who sends his hearers away conscious of a new and deeper impulse of love for their fellow-man has accomplished the highest work.

" If a man love not his brother whom he hath
seen, how can he love God whom he hath not
seen?" This result alone is the test of genuine
spiritual life, It must always be the supreme
result at which every minister must aim, and
one which few do not, in a greater or less
degree, accomplish. However elaborate the
creed or the ritual of any religious organiza-
tion, pastor and people will surely agree that
its essence is love to God and love to man.

" The affections are not private property,
but social energies," says Prof. George D.
Herron, D.D., and he adds : —

" Religion is a social relation. . . . A righteous
society on earth is the kingdom of heaven. . . .
Religion as an absorbent of life is an outrageous im-
position. . . . Jesus came to disclose the divinely
natural order of human life. He never contem-
plated founding the great ethnic religion that bears
his name. It was human life that held him in intensest fascination."

In these words there is to be found a great
illumination on life. Certainly our religion is

a social relation, — unless it is that it is nothing, — but is it not also more? Is it not both a social and a divine relation? A righteous society on earth is the kingdom of heaven; but in order to be a righteous society must it not be fed from that divine realm of higher forces that we call heaven?

No one would more earnestly affirm both these propositions than Dr. Herron. The hearer who could find flaws in the intense moral earnestness of this noble and inspiring speaker would deserve the reward accorded by Apollo to the mortal who sifted the chaff from the wheat by giving him the chaff for his pains.

The one point at which the infinite spirituality, which should be the deepest daily reality of life, separates itself at all from religious socialism is in the mystic nature of the spiritual life. Dr. Herron affirms that man loves mystery, and that God hates mystery. Now the soul's very life *is* mystery, and cannot be translated into ordinary terms; but the ordinary terms may be so exalted as to be transmuted

8

into the glory of this mystery, and the perpetual application of the law of love to life
does, by so much, translate it to that higher
plane of spiritual potency.

When organized worship is a substitute for
human sympathy and love, and for close relations with God, the organized worship must go.
Its service is a means, not an end. But is
this arraignment true? That spiritual ecsta-
sies and rhapsodies are a fraud — as Dr.
Herron asserts — is too true if they end there.
But visions and ecstasy and rhapsody are the
great feeders of the soul. It is in the hour of
consecrated rapture of communion of the soul
with the Holy Ghost that all the energy that
is transmuted into human love and aid is
attained. Here is the great fountain of that
eternal life which we are to realize now if we
hope for it hereafter. The holy mystery of sac-
ramental communion with Christ at the altar
is the intimate renewal of the closest union
of the soul with God. It is not conceivable
that any human being could partake in the
solemn service of the holy communion with-

out a sincere realization of its infinite power.
"Amend your lives and be in charity with all
men : so shall ye be meet partakers of these
holy mysteries. . . . For as the benefit is
great . . . so is the danger great if ye receive
unworthily." Who can kneel and repeat
those words unmoved by their thrilling significance ? Who can live his life in love and
sweetness of human relations only as gained
from periods "in the silence," — periods of
spiritual ecstasy and mystic rhapsody in the
ineffable communion with the Divine Spirit ?
To banish mystery is to banish the source of
spiritual life, for it is the one great mystery.
Most truly should every affection be a social
energy, as Dr. Herron so nobly says. His
message is great and it is needed. Let us
carry into the commonest facts of daily life,
into the street, the market, the social meeting,
every gift and grace of love that can be received through the soul's communion with the
Divine.

Nearly nineteen hundred years have passed
since the Light that shineth more and more

unto the perfect day has come into the world; and that light is now illumination. Side by side with physical evolution has gone a moral evolution. Certain individuals of choice and rare organisms have always lived in the spirit and announced the higher truth to their fellow-men. The number now is multiplying a thousand-fold. All humanity feels the stir and thrill of a new life ; and a large proportion discern it so clearly that the vision of redeemed life on earth — redeemed life here and now — has become a fact accepted as largely as facts of science or data of mathematics. The law of spiritual evolution has brought the universal spirit of man up to that finer degree where he is susceptible to the impression of spiritual truth. That truth is now astir as a redemptive agency throughout the world.

The truth is, that while all the elaborate mechanism of the Church is full of symbolic meaning, and rightly used may be a potent aid to the divine life, it has been regarded too largely as a substitute for that life, and

has acted as a barrier. Formal religion may
be so cold, so impenetrable to sympathy or
claim, so selfish or repellent, as to fairly
cast obloquy on its own name. That it ever
is thus is less true of the present than of the
past; and in this fact lies the great promise
of the future. In an increasing degree the
Church of to-day is alive. "Whatever humanity should do at all the Church should do
supremely," says Rev. Dr. Philip Moxom; and
he adds that if any should heal, the Church
should heal. If there should be gymnasiums
and libraries and social reforms, then the
Church should build gymnasiums and libraries and work social reforms. It is a poor
"spirituality," and something unworthy the
name, that would discard all organized religious life as formal, as lifeless. Not discard,
but re-create, is the true progress. Not separate from the Church, but re-invigorate it and
re-inspire it with advancing ideals. There
was never yet a church or sect or ethical
society which is not large enough for all the
true Christianity that its members or adhe-

rents can live. The higher life of humanity is not to see the downfall of the Church; it is to witness its uplifting, its larger inclusiveness of spiritual ideals.

It can hardly be denied that a flood of new light has poured in on the world from the wide propagation of occult truth. It does not alter, but explains Christianity. Theology as a science never explained the mystery of life with any clearness or coherence to the general intelligence. To "do good" and to live one's own life were largely separable factors until a clearer revelation of the very nature of the soul asserted the truth that to do good *is* life, the only life. The secret of the power of Phillips Brooks was simply that he constantly affirmed this great truth. The only life — the life of all greatness and gladness and gain — is the life of the spirit.

The test of life is to live the days as a poet must, — "to hold the passing day, with its news, its cares, its fears, — to hold it up to a divine reason," till one sees that it has purpose and beauty, and is related to the eternal order of the world.

To be swift to seize the fitting opportunity is to be swift to love. A valuable epigram, embodying the significance of opportunity, is from Kainos, and reads as follows:—

A. Of what town is thy sculptor?

B. Of Likyon.

A. What is his name?

B. Lysippos.

A. And thine?

B. Opportunity, controller of all things.

A. But why standest thou on tiptoe?

B. I am always running.

A. Why, then, hast thou wings on both feet?

B. I fly like the wind.

A. But wherefore bearest thou a razor in thy right hand?

B. As a sign to men that I am sharper than any steel.

A. And why wearest thou thy hair long in front?

B. That I may be seized by him who approaches me.

A. By Zeus! And thou art bald behind?

B. Because, once I have passed with my wingèd feet, no one may seize me there.

A. And for what did thy sculptor fashion
thee?

B. For thy sake, O stranger, and he placed me
in this porch as a lesson. — Auth. Pal., xvi. 295.

Opportunity is a divine gift. The present
day is that in which is heard the announcement of the soul; of that spiritual supremacy
which enters as the controlling and directive
factor into life.

Goodness, in all its various manifestations
of philanthropy, of charity, has been regarded
too much as an accomplishment, an added
grace or achievement, rather than as inherent
in the very texture of life itself. The reward
is not in gratitude received; not even wholly
in the blessed consciousness of having helped
another, but partly, also, in achieving the
higher quality of life itself: as the reward of
study is less in the immediate knowledge
gained than it is in the higher refinement
and larger development of a mind so disciplined by intellectual activities.

Opportunity is responsibility. It is a fleet-
ing conjunction of circumstances. It is a test

as well as a privilege. To be always equal to the opportunity, — what more could be said of the highest success in life? It would con- stitute the noblest success. The one great problem of life, then, resolves itself into this: Is there any way so to live, daily and hourly, that one may always thus be equal to the opportunity that presents itself unexpectedly, and flees if not grasped at once? And if there is such a way, what is it? How can it be found and pursued? On these ques- tions certainly hang the true success, the true happiness of all living.

The conditions of meeting this problem are threefold, and involve body, mind, and soul. They involve, indeed, the complete spirituali- zation of the intellectual and the physical. To draw the line at "the material" is to divorce the working elements of existence. The "material," as we are pleased to call it, is the manifestation of the spiritual, and it is an integral duty of the soul to manifest itself in order, purity, sweetness, and radiance of spiritual sympathy.

Opportunity is well called the controller of all things. The true socialism is the equalization of all privileges. The power to take advantage of them, — that is another matter, and is included in the education and discipline of life.

A great fallacy lies in this: that a vast proportion of opportunities are ruled out as insignificant, and only those that seem to indicate some great deed, something that lifts itself into the visible and the spectacular and of a character to impress mankind, are held as of value. For it is the quality of life that is of importance, and not its specific feats. One salient truth is this, regarding the entire social structure: the things that are in true spiritual correspondence give pleasure, while the same things, when this correspondence is violated, give pain. Now the pain that results from a broken law is to be cherished as a friend and an educator, not regarded as retribution and evil. Wrong-doing goes deeper than even the wrong committed and its results. While

that alone is sufficiently disastrous, it is only
the smallest part of its effects. The greatest
and most disastrous results of any wrong act
are that it forges a link with all the evil of
the universe, and leaves the individual at the
mercy of this crushing and terrible force. An
untruth uttered, an unkind thing said, a mali-
cious deed done, — and lo! one has opened
the door of his life to all the powers of darkness. Disaster and calamity, sustaining no
visible relation to his wrong, are apt to rush
in. The victim often exclaims, "What have
I done to deserve such trouble as this?"
And very probably he has really done nothing that does deserve that specific visitation.
But he has broken a spiritual law, and he
has by that act placed himself in correspondence with evil rather than with good, and so
the forces of evil prevail against him. This is
the wrong use of opportunity.

Conversely, it may be used to open the
gates of all that is beautiful and beneficent.
Good thought connects one with all the forces
of peace, sweetness, and exaltation. Good

fortune is this happy ordering of opportunities. It is the result of connecting the soul
with all the infinite universe of good forces.

Then let us lift up our hearts unto the
Lord. "Lift up your heads, O ye gates,
and be ye lift up, ye everlasting doors, and
the King of Glory shall come in."

*   *   *   *   *

A Servant of the Gods. "I am primarily engaged to myself to be a public servant of all the
gods," writes Emerson; "to demon-
strate to all men that there is good-will and
intelligence at the heart of things, and ever
higher and yet higher leadings. These are my
engagements. If there be power in good
intention, in fidelity, and in toil, the north wind
shall be purer, the stars in heaven shall glow
with a kindlier beam, that I have lived."

There is something not unlike inspiration in
the thought which may come to any young
person on entering a strange city with a view
to making it his home and the scene of his
work and endeavor, that he may contribute to
its progress and enlarge the general scheme of

good. And this not merely by a long probation of toil and economy, or by some exceptional stroke, by means of which he amasses a fortune and uses it for the benefit of society, but even at once, by the forces inherent in himself, which shall ally their strength to all that is noble and thus relate themselves to the factors that make for progress. The sincere and noble nature may assert itself, though it stand alone, penniless, friendless. Even then it may enjoy the luxury of concerning itself with what it may give rather than get. It may keep in sight of its divine inheritance, and realize that its power to range itself with the higher forces is independent of the presence or the absence of material resources.

"I will range myself with the most uplifting forces of the general life." With this resolve the penniless faith is rich, and without it the heir to vast estates is poor.

Now it is a feature of our modern society that there is more need of personal service and personal sympathy than there is of financial endowments. Bequests and contributions

of money are not, after all, especially difficult to secure; but it is sociological Christianity that determines the best uses of
these gifts and relates them to the need of
the day.

Do we not need to realize the truth that
service is inherent in the individual as a
quality of character, and does not necessarily
consist in any specialty of avocation? It is
well that we have our priests who go and live
among the poor; it is well that we have the
men and women who found the social settlement, the dispensary, the free kindergarten,
and the industrial school, — who, in short,
devote themselves to some one department of
service. Yet if these alone serve, humanity
would be far poorer than it is now, not only
in results, but in quality of character. The
true view is that service is the joy-giving
factor in daily life. It is as spontaneous as
light, as subtle as electricity, as exhilarating
as sunshine. It exists primarily as a spiritual
attitude. It lies in the constant recognition
of the brotherhood of humanity toward each

and all with whom we come in contact. The
feeling of kindliness toward the street-car
conductor as one pays his fare, and by word
or expression, or that still more subtle but
equally potent thing we call personal atmosphere, makes him conscious of that kinship of
human brotherhood ; the smile and passing
word with the saleswoman over the counter ;
the very tone in which, perhaps, one refuses to
buy a newspaper of the street boy, — in each
and all this accidental and incidental contact
lie rich possibilities for service. Why should
one reserve his frank good-will, or some spontaneous expression of it, for his personal friends
or the people he believes to be socially important? Why should it not be a part of his
character to radiate happiness unconsciously
as he takes his walks abroad? Good works
do not lie merely — we may even say mostly
— in deeds. They lie in a word, a smile, or
a glance — in that unconscious atmosphere
which each bears about him and communicates. Indeed, the Christianity which does
not manifest itself in love, thoughtfulness,

courtesy, and gentle consideration is not worth
the name.

Its highest power is carried out in faith.
This is too apt to be regarded as an abstract
quality. Never was there a greater error.
Faith is force — a force as positive, as infinite
as electricity. It is a spiritual motor, and as
such is as much more potent than any physical
motor as spirit is more potent than matter.
Material results are controlled and determined
by spiritual causes. Faith without works is
dead, but works without faith are also inert
and lifeless.

Personal happiness is almost synonymous
with personal interests; the wider the range
of the latter the higher is the degree of happiness. Enjoyment, indeed, depends more on
this one faculty of finding a wide and varied
range of sympathies than it does on the possession of fortune, or position, or any other
favorite gifts of circumstance. With the power
of being interested in many things the peasant
is rich, and without it the king is poor. Each
person who can impart to us a new interest in

life is a benefactor; each circumstance that does this is a blessing, however it may be disguised. In Emerson's journal for 1834 there is found this passage: —

"Pray heaven that you may have a sympathy with all sorts of excellence, even with those antipodal to your own. If any eye rests on this page, let him know that he who blotted it could not go into conversation with any person of good understanding without being presently gravelled. The slightest question of his most familiar proposition disconcerted him — eyes, face, and understanding — beyond recovery. Yet did he not the less respect and rejoice in this daily gift of vivacious common-sense which was so formidable to him."

There is a spiritual poverty in the incapacity to feel an interest in other lives than our own that tendeth to destruction. "Excellence encourages us about life generally," says George Eliot. The deepest truth is that extended sympathies draw for their possessor a great increase of strength and magnetism. The vitality of interest in all becomes the concentrated vitality in each. But the deepest prob-

lem, and its most perplexing aspect, is found
in the great gulf that fastidious tastes are apt
to fix between liberal sympathies and their
objects. The penalty of the choicest culture
is inevitable isolation, unless there be moral
greatness, spiritual comprehension, and magnanimity to bridge this gulf. It is proverbially
easier to forgive a crime than a blunder; to
forgive an error of intention rather than a
fault of taste. The more refined is the individual, the more vulnerable are his sensibilities,
and the more easily is he repelled, unless this
refinement be fully balanced by that all-com-
prehending insight and liberal sympathy which
is the result of having achieved a certain culture of the spiritual nature, beyond and above
that of the intellect and the perceptions.
There is a point at which the individual is too
highly polished to be in sympathetic touch
with ordinary life; but there is a far higher
point of accomplishment and mental achievement when the sympathies become so liberal
as to be almost universal in their inclusiveness. That degree of culture whose results

are sterility and aridity of personal life is
certainly not to be greatly esteemed. For
instance, in a home where the average singing
and playing has been a household enjoyment,
a greater degree of musical culture would
transform the pleasure into a torture, while a
yet finer and more perfect culture would create
enjoyment again. There is little doubt that a
joyous appreciation of rather a mediocre type
of art is yet a more healthful and more hopeful state than the carping, critical attitude
that knows enough, indeed, to condemn, but
not enough to create better things than those
it disdainfully discards. Belief is something
good for the soul. That in which it believes
may be very imperfect; but if it serves as a
support until the belief has attained the power
to grasp a higher object, it well fulfils its purpose. Tennyson touches a principle not unlike
this when he says of love : —

> " God gives us love; something to love
> He lends us; but when love is grown
> To its full ripeness, that on which it throve
> Falls off, and love is left alone."

That love is the important thing is true, —
that deep culture of life imparted by the exer-
cise of generous and noble affections : and if
the object be unworthy the offering, it in time
" falls off," and still the charm imparted by
the power of love remains.   And so, " to cultivate a sympathy with all kinds of excellence "
is the one path to the highest personal happiness in life.

It is not by narrow exclusion, by petty,
carping criticism, by doubt and distrust, that
life grows : it is rather by generous faith ; by
a conviction so vital that it creates that in
which it believes; by sympathies so fine that
they include the human with the divine.

It is a curious commentary on life that a
truth-teller is currently supposed to be a person
who sees and says unpleasant things.   " I shall
not flatter you ; *I* shall tell you the truth,"
remarks some self-righteous person, meaning
thereby that you are now to hear a full recount
of all your faults, follies, and failures.   But
even if these assertions be true, they are only
true relatively ; and the one who can see only an

isolated portion of a range of qualities cannot
by any means be said to have grasped truth.
For truth implies wholeness and completeness.
The poet is the best truth-teller, because it is
the poetic temperament alone that has insight
and the illumination of the imaginative gifts.
Mr. Lowell says that good nature is a great
part of good morals; and he is right.

Precisely why sweetness of spirit and good-
will and present appreciation should not be
considered as honest as their reverse in social
intercourse, is not quite clear to the average
mind. Why should a true and sincere appreciation be termed flattery, and degraded to
the level of insincere praise? Why should an
individual be accused of acting from base and
selfish policy because he feels the glow and
warmth of social response? There is as much
pleasant and agreeable truth in the world as
there is of the reverse, — and, indeed, much
more. For that which is sweet and fair and
of good report is much deeper truth than the
unlovely and the evil. Love, in its widest
inclusive and general sense, is the one great

force of the universe. It is the positive, the vital; while all departures from it, in whatever degrees they may be seen, are negation.

The servant of all the gods will resist the natural inclination to restrict his social life to the special circle in which he finds the easy and instinctive comprehension that makes social intercourse thoroughly enjoyable. It is a question if we do not all need the corrective power of miscellaneous society, a variety in our points of view, in order to afford complete adjustment; and it is a still deeper question as to whether it is not impossible to give the best service to society without an intimate personal knowledge of humanity. Is not this where many, who devote their lives unselfishly to what they feel is the highest purpose, fail because of a misconception of values? or lapse into narrow channels because they know only one kind of people, and do not know how the other half live? To associate only with one's co-workers is to fail of receiving the light of criticism thrown on any project by its opponents. The philanthropist, the worker for humanity in any direction, has need of personal contact with the social grades apart from his own.

Lives are enlarged in different ways; both by the culture of art and polite society, and also by contact with the common and untrained. Mental vistas are secured from a deeper knowledge of all kinds of people. No one liveth unto himself. No one, who is not hopelessly narrow and selfish, can isolate himself from the great inter-relations of human experience.

The more one cultivates liberality of sympathies the more varied and stimulating is the entire panorama of social life. The more largely life can be related to all phases of society, the more deeply and nobly may it be lived.

*   *   *   *   *

The Ethics of Journalism. The assumption that journalism, the greatest of modern forces, is a matter of art and of ethics, is one that can hardly fail to be conceded by the reader; for the finer civilization in

which we are beginning to live, and which
is at once the cause and the effect of finer
forces, demands artistic form and ethical purpose as the vital factors of every great achievement. In no expression of life is this fact
more clearly shown than in journalism. For,
indeed, when we come to scrutinize this all-
pervasive force, this marvellous influence
which, by remoulding and directing the individual, is shaping the national destiny, we
see its claim is that of life itself, and we
recognize that newspapers have souls, whatever may be said of corporations. The newspaper is not only the contemporary, but it is
the magic mirror, turned forward ; and it shows
us not only what is, but what should be. The
actual and the ideal meet in its pages. There
is a very mistaken notion sometimes enter-
tained by persons who are, or who believe
themselves to be, " literary," — and thus of a
finer clay than the journalist, — that the minimum of newspaper reading and the maximum
of that in books is the predestined path to
glory, and that this proportion of the two in-

gredients promote that state which they are
pleased to call " culture."

Mr. Andrew Lang placed himself on record
to this effect: " Do read good books, and
don't read magazines and newspapers ; " which
advice, if literally followed, would deprive us
of the most immediate sources of current information, and even of a certain per cent of
pure literary enjoyment, as, for instance, the
missing of Mr. Lang's oracular counsel, which
is materialized through the magazines. The
autocratic and not altogether discriminating
manner in which Mr. Lang draws the line, indicates in how slight a degree he has related
himself to the present currents of thought.
Good books are certainly great reservoirs of
wisdom from which to draw. But because
one is familiar with the psychological problems
that tortured Hamlet, or the circles that Dante
saw, is no assurance that he will be competent
to cast a vote on matters of importance in his
city if he does not read the daily newspapers.
To say that a man does not gain in intellectual
strength and moral poise by being on familiar

terms with the best ancient and modern
classics, would be manifestly untrue; but to
say that even the greatest literature of the
past can wholly supply the needs of to-day is
equally remote from the truth. The fact is,
that the modern newspaper is the true "heir
of all the ages." Like Bacon, it has taken all
knowledge to be its province. Our leading
daily papers are cosmopolitan in their afflu-
ence of knowledge. All foreign movements,
diplomacy, religion, and society, are reflected
each day in their pages; every new invention;
every great discovery or new theory in science;
every great achievement in art or literature;
our own political life; contemporary biography; criticism and imaginative literature,
beside all that daily miscellany vaguely de-
nominated the "news," are given semi-daily,
and the vast enterprise and energy, the discrimination in intellectual values, and the
moral purpose controlling this gigantic and
complicated profession, may certainly merit
the serious attention of a learned and thoughtful association.

To read the semi-daily and Sunday issues of any great journal is to have an admission ticket to the entire panorama of the world every day. The symmetry and balance of perfection observed in its presentation of foreign and domestic matter, its literary features, criticism, correspondence, and art, are marvels of achievement, and its daily reading offers a liberal education.

Mr. John Morley, in his essay on "The Study of Literature," says that the supreme object of all is to make good citizens. How can a man be a good citizen who has neither knowledge of current affairs nor interest in their tendency?

> "And, for success, I ask no more than this,
> To bear unflinching witness to the truth."

What can we say of success in life, — that noble success which is not merely that of personal gain, but of general advancement, — that is truer than these words? And how can one "bear unflinching witness to the truth" who knows little and cares less what the truth of to-day is to us?

To the public each important newspaper
comes to have its individuality. Its sentiment has the force of a personal expression,
with the added emphasis inherent in the
printed form. The ideal newspaper pre-sup-
poses such a selection and grouping of work
as blend into a complete unity. Its editorial
page is no collection of "unrelated frag-
ments," as Clarence Cook declared the Ces-
nola antiquities to be, but an arrangement
of brief and well-considered essays, which,
while isolated by the special subject treated,
find a harmony in general tendency and trend
of thought. The personal feeling of the writer
is held amenable to the journalistic ideal of
the paper. In Mr. Howells's "Modern Instance," he portrays the seamy side of journalism; but although "The Events" and the
"Chronicle-Abstract" of that entertaining
novel-writer may not be without their pro-
totypes in actual life, they are no represen-
tatives of modern journalism. The newspaper
whose conduct and convictions are merely a
matter of traffic could in this day enter upon

no prosperous or permanent career. With a journal, as with the individual, honesty is very sure to be the best policy, even considering the law of rectitude from the point of expediency alone. No Bartley Hubbard could win success in our best modern journalism, because it demands character as well as capacity on the part of the journalist. But a novelist has his privileges, and we should not require of him the statistical accuracy of the biographer. We will forgive much to a novel that delights us, even if it is a little unfair to one of the noblest of the professions. A newspaper is an affair of business, it is true, and not alone of sentiment; and still there is that in its nature and tendencies which constantly introduces higher motives than financial gain alone. Dealing with humanity and with events, — which are the materialized expression of humanity, — it comes into the essential atmosphere of idealism, as distinguished from mere materialism. Its very responsibility educates the moral sense of those who contribute to its forces. It is a law of ethics that the more one feels the inter-dependence, the subtle relations of humanity, the more scrupulously will he endeavor to repress in himself all selfish and unworthy tendencies, and stimulate to a higher growth his better impulses and truer recognitions.

Reportorial work offers the young journalist a great school both for information and for development. His university training, or its substitute, has given him its tools; reportorial journalism teaches him how to handle them, — lectures, conventions, trips of observation here and there, with ways and means made easy: his work being its own introduction to notable people, it is evident that reportorial work is largely, as Mrs. Browning said of poetry, its "own exceeding great reward." In fact, so far as opportunities go, the next best thing for a young man who is not the son of a rich man is to be a reporter on an enterprising daily newspaper. The "next best" does one say? Ah, is not the work which stimulates every power of mind and heart the best, rather than the life whose privileges require no corresponding duties?

The vocation of literary journalism is one beginning to be widely recognized as offering an important field for usefulness; as one that is especially educative to its followers, congenial to the individual of literary tastes, and which has the advantage over magazine contributing or book-making in furnishing an immediate support by means of a definite weekly salary. The one important article of faith for the literary journalist is to believe, with the utmost depth of conviction, that there is nothing too good for the daily newspaper, and the one anxiety is to secure that which is good enough for it. The influence the press exerts on the lives of the American people is simply incalculable. The daily newspaper is a mill whose constant grist must be supplied. It is constantly demanding an advance of quality in the matter it publishes. Its work is, for the class, permanent; for the individual, often, though by no means always, transient. A competent newspaper writer will

never, it is safe to say, lack for good work and
sure pay.   But when one uses the word competent, it is with a significance before which
he trembles, and asks, "Who is sufficient for
these things?"   The successful newspaper
writer must give to the work that eternal
vigilance which is not alone the price of lib-
erty, but the price of almost everything worth
having in this world.   Work on the daily
press must never be considered as a trade, a
mechanism, a pursuit to be chosen at will and
for what it will bring, rather than for what
the aspirant can bring to it.   It requires a
certain creative type of talent to be an accept-
able newspaper writer; and writers who are
asking the question, "Does it pay?" will find
more immediately important questions to ask
before it will pay them.   Like all forms of
literary work, journalism to a large degree
chooses its votaries rather than waits to be
chosen by them.   The essential aim of journalism is less what one can get out of it than
what one can put into it; that is, it is especially the work which may be made a per-

sonal contribution to one's day and generation. All earnest, thinking men and women live for something higher than greed, or getting, or gain, and in every privilege opened by the horizon of journalism there is found a corresponding duty. In this way journalists are contributing to the intellectual and social progress of the world.

The discipline of the local work on a city daily is simply invaluable. Later, if the worker shall make the constant intellectual growth demanded for editorial work, he has the technique of the profession, and is fitted for it. Editorial work presupposes acquirement, ready knowledge, and all the culture to which one should have grown. The editorial writer begins a day knowing not what news will flash upon the world to be intelligently and rapidly discussed. In the flash of a moment may come the news that the Czar of all the Russias has been assassinated, that Darwin, George Eliot, the Emperor Frederick, Cardinal Newman, Tennyson, are dead; and fact and history, and intelligent comprehension and clear thought,

10

must meet and mingle to prepare the comments for the press. There is then no time for library research. The journalist must not only have knowledge, but that knowledge must be instantly available.

The personal qualities that make one a favorite guest in the drawing-room are not less indispensable in the newspaper office, — the same sweetness of spirit, refinement, tact, and sympathetic comprehension, with the added obligation of energy and reliability. Opportunities correspond with almost mathematical accuracy to the ability for using them. Fitness for any work creates its own theatre of action. That eternal vigilance which is the price of success will exact of the journalist three essentials, — good health, constant literary study, and study of life. Health is more largely a mental and moral as well as a physical condition than we altogether realize, and it has a very intimate connection with good sleep. However other people live, the journalist must live for his art, and live the life of the artist. If he would bring to his

morning work clearness of thought, balance
of judgment, and that nervous force necessary to establish the circuit between brain
and hand, he must insist on good sleep, avoid
late suppers and excitements that absorb all
nervous force and leave one drifting help-
lessly at the mercy of demands rather than
to be able by vitality and vigor to command
the situation.   Social recreation is one thing;
social dissipation is quite another.   Fortunately for one who, like the journalist, must
so live as to find his energies and powers
available in the morning, and who cannot
yet isolate himself from the tides and forces
of active life, — fortunately for him there is a
constantly advancing tendency toward earlier
hours in the social world.   So, as far as social
life goes, there seems no positive necessity for
late hours, even though one enjoy most of the
entertainments, public and private; and early
sleep is a condition that must positively be
insisted on by one who desires to do strong
and enduring journalistic work.   If he con-
ceives of journalism in the light of the cari-

cature of itself, — as the mere writing of
personal events, fashion notes, and light gos-
sip, — it will matter less out of what condition
of mind or body they are written; if he desire
a wide outlook, earnest thought, and elevated
purpose, it matters very greatly.

Again, there is the duty of reading, — not
alone the pleasure of it, but the absolute duty;
and it is important for one who would succeed in journalism. Libraries are those un-
failing fountains to which one goes to be
filled. Reading is indeed to the mind as
is food to the body, — the material of which
its fibre is made. It is surprising to note the
difference in the quality of mental thought
which even one-half hour's good reading each
day will make; and to the man who has vol-
untarily entered journalism as a profession,
and assumed the responsibility of certain work,
it is a matter of ethics to keep himself in mental condition to respond to the work and fulfil
its demands.

There is also the importance of keeping in
touch with life. No exclusive bookworm can

ever be a successful journalist. If press work is anything it is vital, and the successful conductor of it must be alive to his finger-tips, and keep in touch with the current of affairs. There is a centripetal tendency in work on the daily newspapers which he who would command the situation must counteract by excursions without; by dipping into new atmospheres, and seeing life under new skies. To touch life at all points; to touch it with some perception of its ideal possibilities and of its actual realizations, and to hold the golden mean of fidelity to noble standards and charity for imperfect results, is the education in that experience which makes wisdom.

The phrase "personal journalism" is currently accepted in its narrowest limits and most frivolous possibilities; but this is not its true scope. What, indeed, is all biography, and to a great degree all history, but personal writing? What makes the charm of the novel save personal interests dramatically presented? National and international politics take their color and their importance from the personalities of the men who are the prime movers; and since the world in general is made for men and women and is made by them, the personal element cannot be eliminated from that which is the expression of a people's life — its journalism. That it is sometimes degrading and corrupting, and should be eliminated, is true; and it is also true that there is already a perceptible tendency in this direction. Perhaps the worst aspect of the demand for personal journalism is the temptation it offers a class of writers to sacrifice individual honor and integrity to a temporary gain. They may come in possession of some of those essentially private and personal facts of a man's life which it would be a matter of ideal integrity to refrain from circulating. If related to the journalist as matter of friendly confidence, the obligation is sufficiently obvious; if they chance to come to his knowledge through indirect means, the obligation is not less strong because it is more subtle and more entirely an affair of honor. But the current of the journalistic maelstrom

which craves sensation draws him in almost, it
may be, imperceptibly; he cheats himself with
plausible sophistries; he declares that if he
does not "get ahead of the other fellow," and
give it in the "Rambler" to-day, it will be
snapped up and elaborated in the "Tattler" to-
morrow. He knows such matter is instantly
available in cash, and so sells his soul for a
mess of pottage. Yet, to the credit of journalism be it said, such success — if the term
may be so desecrated — is as transient as it is
trivial. The journals that will publish and
pay for such dishonorable work do not respect
the man who will lend himself to do it. In
time, and usually, too, not a very long time,
he loses his position, and loses all that respect
which makes life worth the living. Journalistic reputation is good, but journalistic character is better. Its success is, after all, but
the fine inflorescence of life, which is the fruit
that many conditions go to perfect. Temperament, the power of sympathetic assimila-
tion, versatile availability, sweetness of spirit,
the faculty to live harmoniously in the atmos-

phere of a newspaper office which is a world of itself, and professional enthusiasm, — all these are indispensable factors in success, and without these qualifications the mere ability to write acceptably will never make a professional journalist.

Journalism should be truthful. It should insist that shams are not entitled to public confidence and support; it should insist, even at the risk of being held unsympathetic and unkind, that the person who needs or desires to do remunerative work shall enter on it by honest and legitimate effort.

The requirements of literary journalism, measured by its ideal standard, are far greater than those required for the irregular production of specific literary contributions to periodicals.

The literary journalist must perforce take all knowledge for his province to a great degree. His ideal work implies behind it the endeavor to realize noble ideals. No great and permanent work comes out of narrow and trivial life.

The degree of achievement in literary journalism will be determined more by the individual inclinations, aspirations, and ideals of the journalist, than by the time, place, or circumstances of outer life. For it is one of the eternal laws that the real life — that which is permanent and determining — depends little on external scenery. The spirit fashions its own world, regardless of visible correspondence between its inner visions of beauty and its actual environment of limitations or even deprivations. Fortunately, poverty of the purse does not necessarily produce poverty of the spirit. Life may be so hedged in by circumstances as to be narrow, but may always be deep and high. And it is depth that gives enduring power, and it is height that affords an outlook.

It is important that the journalist should adequately recognize his responsibility as a public trust. There may be a conspicuous effacement and ignoring of self that is not true humility, but is more like egoism ; there may be a consciousness of self that hinders. Between these extremes he must seek that degree which is no mere ambition for personal aggrandizement, but which counts ambition as worthy only as a means to bring his message to the hour and the time. Archdeacon Farrar says that the remedy for our social difficulties is to be found "in the manly and heroic determination of all good men, whatever may be the position, that, so far as they are concerned, no effort shall be left untried which seems to offer the least chance of improving the conditions of our national life, and raising strong hands to bring heaven a little nearer to this our earth." Canon Farrar dwells on the individual responsibility in this struggle against vice and misery, and refers to the example of the Grecian soldiers, who, as related by Greek historians, thought in a decisive battle that unless they were individually fighting the great cause would be lost. There is a suggestion in this well worthy the consideration of the journalist.

"It may be glorious to write
  Thoughts that shall glad the two or three
High souls, like those far stars that cause sight
  Once in a century : —

"But better far it is to speak
  One simple word, which now and then
Shall waken their free nature in the weak
  And friendless sons of men :

"To write some earnest verse or line
  Which, seeking not the praise of art,
Shall make a clearer faith and manhood shine
  In the untutored heart.

"He who doth this, in verse or prose,
  May be forgotten in his day,
But surely shall be crowned at last with those
  Who live and speak for aye."

VIBRATIONS.

If you once feel the inward power of vibrations you
will never go back. There is no such thing as going
from light to darkness. When the Ancients pictured
their god of day as making music with the strings of a
musical instrument, it was but a prefiguring of what
is coming now to every one who has taken possession
of his birthright as Son of God. . . . When the heart
alone is sending forth its vibratory waves, we receive
into our innermost being the very essence of life. As
the desire goes forth on the unseen wires, reaching out
for God, there will meet it the return wave of divine
melody, and thus interpenetrating we are fed by God
and nourished into the real life. — *Zenia.*

Moreover, something is or seems,
That touches me with mystic gleams,
Like glimpses of forgotten dreams —

Of something felt, like something here;
Of something done, I know not where ;
Such as no language may declare. — TENNYSON.

"It so chanced
On that leaden-hearted day,
Rugged Winter leagues away,
As he thought of her there came
On the waste a sunny flame
Where within the frost-mote danced,
· While an echo rang her name.
It so chanced."

SELF–CONTROL AND PLEASANT SPEECH.

Much insight and education,
Self-control and pleasant speech,
And whatever word be well spoken ;
This is the greatest blessing.

— GAUTAMA, THE BUDDHA.

"SELF–CONTROL and pleasant speech" are all-conquering forces. Pleasant speech has its source in pleasant feeling, and this generates that harmony which is the first condition of both individual and social achievement. This harmony, the faculty to "get on" well with people, is a gift and a grace. The individual who always has a grievance becomes simply impossible. If one of his pet theories of the malice prepense of his next-door neighbor, or the depravity of humanity in general, is disproved or explained away to his possible satisfaction, a dozen more equally elaborate and

intricate grievances spring up in its place, requiring also to be elucidated. Such tasks become hopeless. The individual who cultivates
grievances and who is perpetually exacting
explanations of his assumed wrongs can only
be ignored, and left to the education of time
and of development. To recognize his delu-
sions even to the extent of argument, is only
to confirm him in irritable and exacting conditions ; in low and pernicious moral states.
One does not argue or contend with the foul
miasma that settles over stagnant water ; one
leaves it and climbs to a higher region, where
the air is pure and the sunshine fair. It
is only the stagnant pool that breeds slime
and noxious vapors ; the swift-running water
is clear and pure. And so, if one finds himself degenerating into an irritable or bitter or
morbid state, let him seek the currents of
spiritual activity, and the atmosphere will
grow clear again.

"Insight and education ! " "Self-control
and pleasant speech ! " These are, indeed,
the keys to happiness, and that success which

is included in happiness. "Let us live happily, not hating those who hate us," the high precepts continue. "Let us live happily, though we call nothing our own," — for then, indeed, shall we "become like the bright gods that feed on happiness." The entire ingredients of the exaltation which we call happiness are spiritual. Happiness is a spiritual state. One may be in conditions that he does not like; he may be forced to do things that he would not choose to do, or to refrain from doing what he might choose, — but that is a mere incident. Conditions are fluid in their capacity for change. They are plastic. Sufficient spiritual force brought to bear can transform adverse conditions into more favorable aspects; but this is not done by fret or worry or irritable rebellion. Antagonism is negative, and only disintegrates. Faith and vision and sweetness of spirit are the creative forces that transform one set of conditions into another. Surely we may live happily though we call nothing our own. "A man's life consisteth not in the abundance of the things which he

11

possesseth." Let us "feed on happiness;" let us live in exaltation and sunshine, and thus become like "the bright gods."

If this were mere rhetoric, it would not be worth the writing nor the reading. But it is the most absolutely practical doctrine of human life. Sweetness of spirit radiates outwardly in vibrations which, more subtle than the vibrations of light or heat, are also more potent. They are more powerful in their action on conditions, and in the impression they convey to others, than even the highest force of which we know — electricity. That mental states produce these vibrations is as exact data as that of any physical science. Chemical changes are not more absolutely demonstrable than are these. They act on conditions as the sun's rays act upon snow to melt and dissipate it, or as light acts upon darkness — which flees before the sun. So do all dark conditions and dreary circumstances flee before the vibrations of the radiant, trusting, hopeful, and serenely sweet spirit.

The study of occult laws is the study of

life. This study is to every one what the chart of navigation is to the seaman. Learning the principles of navigation, he guides his ship without this knowledge he is at the mercy of wind and wave. The time has now come when humanity is to grasp the principles of right living; when it is to learn the science and nature of the soul.

Spirit is the one most potent force; and so far as one learns to live in the spirit, he learns to control the conditions of his life. Karma is not blind, irresistible fate, but is one factor only, which a stronger spiritual force may counteract and change. " Self-control and pleasant speech " — the radiant faith that grasps ideal conditions, realizes them also in outward living.

Spirituality is not a luxury or a decorative appendage of life, to be occasionally displayed. It is the practical power of daily living. It is the force that achieves, the force that succeeds. Nothing is more disastrous than to fall into the habit of complaint and grievances. If things go wrong, bridge over the defect

by laying hold resolutely on higher states.
Transmute falsehood to truth, irritability to
pleasant speech, doubt and distrust to faith.
So shall one " feed on happiness."

" Let us live happily, then, not hating those who hate
    us !
  Let us live happily, then, though we call nothing our
    own !
  We shall become like the bright gods who feed on
    happiness."

Only that life is rich which never misses
an opportunity to do a kindness. Whether
this kindness is shown to the rich or the
poor, the great or the unknown, is of very
little consequence, and is, indeed, a matter
beyond our rightful province. It is one's
responsibility as well as privilege to take advantage of every opportunity as it presents
itself; and the way these opportunities multiply in daily life, if one is swift to recognize
them, is one of the most interesting facts in
the entire panorama of living. The woman
who remarked that she never minded her own
business but once in her life and then she

was sorry for it, had grasped the right clue to living. For one's "own business" is a very elastic term. It includes far more than one's personal concerns. It is a part of individual responsibility that reaches out in many and in varied directions. The person who interprets his "own business" to mean nothing beyond his personal affairs will find himself living a very narrow, hard, selfish, and colorless life. If his neighbor has any need of "mind, body, or estate" that he can meet, there lies a part of his "own business." If his neighbor is cold or hungry or ill clad, and he can relieve him, wholly or in part, there is his business. If there are needs, or sorrows, or anxieties, — less visible and tangible, but even more real, because they involve mental or spiritual suffering, — there lies his own business. One may well turn from all his personal concerns and devote his utmost energy and his time and his power of thought to meeting an emergency or need in the life of his neighbor. Whoever needs him is his neighbor. The term does not designate material proximity, but spiritual relation.

The higher plane of Christian living will not, indeed, ever be reached until the clumsy methods of public philanthropy shall give place to the subtle and sympathetic methods of private and personal service. Doing good should not need to be a profession, an occupation separable and separate from ordinary life; it should be the natural, spontaneous accompaniment of the hourly and daily living. It is really not necessary that, in order to assist in serving humanity, one should migrate to some new locality and advertise his purpose, either *viva voce* or by a poster. To do good should be the spiritual condition, and not in the least a matter of geography. As things go now, public and professional philanthropies are far better than no philanthropies at all; and it is far better to migrate across a city and found a social settlement than it is to live in selfish indifference to the needs of the less fortunate. But the time will come when formal charities will be so superseded by

the spontaneous and all-pervading love and
sympathy, in simple and natural relations, that
organized municipal efforts will be superfluous.
If each individual in the world simply did all
that was in his power each day for the persons whose lives come in natural contact with
his own, — whether in the relations of servants, or friends, or acquaintances, or stran-
gers, — the entire world would be regenerated
at once. Nor need this interfere in the least
with his ordinary work and pursuits. Everything is possible to courtesy and to love.
They are spiritually expansive, and, like the
miracle of the loaves and the fishes, the more
they are given, the more they increase. The
more they are divided, the more they are
multiplied. There are certain things that,
done for another, consume time and strength,
but — if done out of the loving impulse,
this time and strength will be transmuted
by some divine alchemy into renewed energies,
which will give him infinitely greater impetus
in his own special work. Indeed, his individual work can safely be trusted, if the

call to action elsewhere comes to him. It is
he that loseth his life who shall find it.
These words are not a mere rhetorical phrase,
but they stand for the profoundest and most
practical truth. The "laying up treasures in
heaven" is simply the creating of spirituality
by holding the thought and doing the deed
that is generous and loving. It is by means
of this phase of achievement and this quality
of atmosphere that we extend our domain into
the spiritual world.

The one great truth is that we need to
divest ourselves of the idea that doing good
is a matter of self-sacrifice and martyrdom.
On the contrary, it is the only condition of
completeness of life. It is the bloom, the
flower, the fruit. All else is rudimentary,
and this is the condition of inflorescence.

> "Make my mortal dreams come true
> With the good I fain would do;
> If there be a weaker one,
> Give me strength to help him on;
> Clothe with life the weak intent:
> Let me be the thing I meant."

*   *   *   *   *

The Threefold Forces.

To do always and everywhere the best we know at the moment, — this surely would be to lead the ideal · life. Now the moment one relegates this idea to the realms of the impossible, — considering an ideal to be merely a superfluous luxury rather than the most practical and immediate necessity of daily life, — that moment he accepts the ignoble for the noble, the trivial for the great, the insignificant for the significant, the inconsequential for the important. If to do one's best at one given moment is possible, — and that will freely be admitted by every one, — then to do one's best always is equally possible, provided one holds himself continually to the higher plane of living. And this involves the threefold quality of physical, mental, and spiritual life. All physical culture rests on the great truth that to refine the body, to render it more sensitive, more plastic, more intelligent, — for intelligence is not limited to the brain, but is carried by the nerves to every portion of the body, — to thus educate and train the physical system is to prepare the conditions for a more significant life. The end of physical culture is not to be an athlete, but to be a more thoughtful, just, generous, considerate, and efficient individual. It is this higher life — of greater unity, of more complete symmetry — for which all physical culture stands. Science tells us that "the brain is not the originator of perceptions, impressions, or thoughts, but a receptive and reactive agent, or rather one of several centres, so completely enveloping human anatomy that nowhere on the surface of the body can so much as the point of a pin be placed without coming in contact with it."

This emphasizes the truth that the initial power of living the day to one's best each moment is to enter on it aright with the threefold preparation of the threefold being. The morning bath, the proper food for breakfast, and the theme of one's meditation and prayer, determine the course of the day. Thought is the most potent of magnets; and it can be brought to a degree of determining influence as yet undreamed of, even by the seer or the prophet. After one has completed his toilet, after the morning meditation and prayer, let him still, before leaving his room and coming in contact with the currents of life, take a little time to realize the day that lies before him fair as an unwritten page. In these moments of realization he can, if he comprehend the mystic potency that is his, absolutely create the day. He can determine all its tendencies; he can shape its events; he can control the elements that await the psychic stamp of his individuality. He may live intelligently, divinely, as well as to merely drift ignorantly. Not only is it his privilege, but his duty. Wherefore is man an intelligent and reasonable being save that he is to use his intelligence and ally himself with the divine forces of the universe? Let one in the early morning, while yet alone in his room, centralize his thought. Let him realize that he is a co-worker with God; that he is in this world to co-operate with the divine purpose; that it is in the line of his higher duty and his sweetest privileges to

radiate a charmed atmosphere of sweetness,
of helpful thought, of good-will, and of love to
every one he meets, to all with whom he
comes in contact. Success lies in the quality
of the life lived, of this power of radiating
courage and earnestness and joy, of the ability
to communicate this impulse. That is what
life is for — for mutual spiritual benefit. In
this lies the "holy earnestness," which, as
Goethe truly says, "alone makes life eternity."

To do the best for one day, on each occasion that presents itself, makes it the more
possible for the next day. Science has dis-
covered that every act records itself on the
brain, and that it thus grows in accordance
with the quality of action impressed on it
until a given line of conduct becomes so ha-
bitual that it is fairly automatic.

Simple as it sounds, the doing one's best at
each moment is all there is of life. To do
one's best with that supreme spiritual energy
thus generated is to transform the entire range
and scenery of life. The statisticians tell us
about "prisoners of poverty;" but the only

real prisoners are those of thought, — those
who have not yet learned how to think, and
who do not know that the power of right
thought is the most powerful dynamo. There
is no conceivable barrier of circumstances that
it will not batter down and annihilate. It
transforms illness to health, inactivity to
energy, monotony to the most intensely interesting and ecstatic zeal, limitations and
trial to largeness of circumstances and outlook, and to the utmost beauty and charm
of life.

Paul Tynan well says: —

"It is by doing always and everywhere the best
we know that such doing becomes the natural,
easy, and pleasant habit, and character is formed.
Every experience, every impulse, every emotion
leaves a physical record and tendency in the brain
and nervous system as a whole, — that is to say, in
the man. The different parts or areas of the brain
are thus developed, and what was potential becomes
real."

A common discouragement, however, is this,
— that in the life of every one who has really

tried to make his life something finer and
nobler, and more impressive in its influence
than a mere existence could be, there come
retrogressions, backward eddies in the tide,
unforeseen obstacles and hindrances. What
then? Shall he give up the struggle and
relapse into commonplace activities? "There
is no sorrow I have thought more about than
this," wrote George Eliot: "that one who
aspires to live a higher life than the common should fall from that serene height into
the soul-wasting struggle with worldly annoyances." Nor is there any sorrow, or loss, or
pain of life equal to this experience. To deny
it would be false; to ignore it would be
foolish. It is one which may come to any of
us, which does come to many of us, and it is
not blindness that will aid, but rather the
clearer sight to recognize the experience at its
true value; to hold the serenity of spirit that
will not be unduly terrified and thus exaggerate the evil, and also the seriousness of con-
templation that will not flippantly pass it by.

The mysterious principle of vicarious atonement has prevailed in the universe, and revealed itself, in some form, through every age and in every national and individual history. The Christ on Calvary is but the supremest, divinest form that the truth has taken. The Roman legend that tells us how Curtius leaped into the dark gulf that closed over him is but another attestation of the way this universal truth has taken root in every literature and every land. No work, not even the individual work of one's own life, is ever assured until sacrifice, in some form or other, is made. "That which thou sowest is not quickened except it die." It is the power to recognize this relation of temporary defeat to eternal success which is the all-determining factor; the power to see, — not the mere paltry annoyances of the moment, but the vision shining fair beyond, — and to endure, as seeing Him who is invisible.

To recognize loss, or pain, or annoyance — not as things to regard flippantly, not as facts to exaggerate — is to assume the conquering attitude. No one is defeated until he gives

up. The point is then not to give up. Life
is, after all, a supernatural affair, an affair of
supernaturalism, and it is the invisible powers
which are its stay, its guide, and its inspiration.
We live and move and have our being on the
divine side of things. We only live — in any
true sense — as we are filled with the heavenly
magnetism. "Thou hast made known to me
the ways of life; thou shalt make me full of
joy with thy countenance," says the apostle.
Here is the true gospel to live by. There *are*
"ways of life;" even through toil and trial
they shall be reached. The one is eternal,
the other temporal. It is unwise to lay too
much stress on the infelicities of the moment.
Exaltation alone is real: depression is unreal.
The obstacle is not intended to stop progress,
but to stimulate new energies.

> "And he who flagged not in the earthly strife
> From strength to strength advancing — only he
> His soul will knit, and all his battles won,
> Mounts and that hardly to eternal life."

For one mounts to eternal life — now. Not
in some vague to-morrow, but to-day. Eter-

nal life is a condition, not a period. Live in immortal energies, in noble purpose, in true uplift of soul, and one lives at once, and here, the immortal life. His soul has already put on immortality.

Trial and perplexity teach one the wiser meanings of life, and the way to speed their departure is to grasp the meaning as swiftly as possible. Then demand from the higher powers the aid to overcome this plane and to live upon that where all work is done with exhilaration. It will be given in even greater measure than one could ask.

It is these matters that are now those of chief concern to the public in general. It is a very striking fact that of all the long series of congresses held in Chicago in connection with the World's Exposition none began to attract such crowds and throngs as those which discussed religion and the higher life. The psychical, the theosophical, and the great Parliament of Religions — a sublime assembly — were those to which the people thronged in a degree tenfold greater than to those de-

12

voted to science or economics. For the whole
world is feeling the electric thrill of a new
life. Our Sinai is before us, and we realize
that we must climb it and hold converse with
the Divine. A wave of new invigoration is
sweeping over the entire world. The gospel
of hope, of faith, is bearing men to a wingèd
vantage ground.

To keep one's feet firmly set in the way
that leads upward, however dark and thorny it
may be at the moment, is to conquer. Annie
Besant, in an eloquent address before the
Theosophical Congress, made the impressive
statement that years devoted to dealing with
problems of the lower planes of life had made
her believe that the employment of one hour
daily, in spiritual energy for the laborer, works
more good than one hundred years of material processes for relief.

"For instance," she said, "the thought is
first evolved, then imaged in the astral light,
then precipitated into action and material
effort. It is only because we are blinded that
we lay so much stress on the action and so

little to the mental cause." Here is the true secret of success.

All trial is in its very nature temporal; all joy is in its nature eternal. Legions of angelic powers wait upon the soul and guide it to the Mount of Vision.

*   *   *   *   *

Omens traced in Air. " For what need I of book or priest,
Or sibyl from the mummied East,
When every star is Bethlehem star?"

The old adage, " Make the best of things," is grounded in occult wisdom. That is to say, Never quarrel with Fate. Make friends with circumstances. Bring yourself into harmony with your surroundings. For the links of fate and circumstance that impel one onward to a certain course have all their cause and their sequence, and even if they seem adverse, must be worked through and not worked against. Thought is the most potent form of creative force. The scriptures say, " As a man thinketh, so is he." And so, as one thinks his surroundings or circumstances are, so do they become.

When the unexpected happens, make friends
with it. Something has been taken away that
one cares for very much; but the very fact
that one thing is removed makes room for
something else. If one is wise, he will fix his
thought on the new possibilities and develop
them into new and satisfying combinations.
The old way is closed. The avenue is hedged
in, and he must seek a new path. But why
repine? There is more than one way, and the
unknown one may offer vistas yet undreamed
of, and prospects full of enchantment.

"Who can answer where any road leads
to?"

If one loses a thing that is good, — whether
it be his home, or his place for a certain work,
or one thing or another that has made up the
locale or the scenery of his accustomed life, —
let him not confront the changed prospect
with regret or dismay. "If your hands are
left empty," said Emerson, "it is only that
they may seek and hold better gifts."

It is not a sign of power, but of weakness,
when one clings obstinately to old conditions.

There is always a time for changes to come, and not infrequently is it a date wholly unforeseen. But however unfortunate the change may seem, — make friends with the new conditions. Vitalize them with hope and faith and love; thus shall a magnetic atmosphere be generated that shall draw to itself all those qualities which are hoped for, and of whose existence one holds clear convictions. The new home, the new work, the new circumstances and conditions, — they are depressing, narrow, undesirable. All the more, then, may one make them desirable, and call up spirits from the vasty deep to invest them with enchantment.

For life is not being lived according to its best possibilities unless lived with the thrill and exaltation of happiness. One should do one's work in a state of exhilaration. The days should be high and beautiful and poetic. They should be peopled with imaginations and enthusiasms. "Every touch should thrill," said Emerson; and only in this intense yet serene exaltation is there achieved the better possibilities that may be daily realized by each and all.

And this is achieved by escaping from the material into the spiritual. Man is a divine being, and he should live daily and hourly the divine life. Anything less than that defrauds him of his inheritance. Not "in the separation of the soul from the body," as Dr. Anna Kingsford says, — "not in the separation of the soul from the body, but in the purification of both soul and body from engrossment by the things of sense."

Almost all the things that we call misfortune are of material loss or failure. Yet one should consider it a far greater misfortune if he said what was untrue, or if he had been unkind or inconsiderate, or selfish, or dishonorable. In these would lie his real calamity, because by these acts he is impairing and undermining the quality of his spiritual life, which is his essential life. It may be a severe inconvenience to lose money, or to lose any or all of the material resources to which he is accustomed; but it is only an inconvenience, not a misfortune.

The great desiderata are to be found in the entire spiritualization of life. "By living so purely in thought and in deed as to prevent the interposition of any barrier between his phenomenal and substantial self; and by steadfastly cultivating harmonious relations between these two — by substantiating the whole of his system to the Divine Central Will, whose seat is in the soul, — the man gains full access to the stores of knowledge laid up in his soul, and attains to the cognition of God and the universe. . . . Revelation is, no less than reason, a natural appanage of man, and belongs of right to man in his highest and completest measure of development."

All this divine inheritance of treasures of wisdom, of knowledge, of love, of beauty, is the natural daily life. If one does not partake of its infinite resources he is not living aright. Let him make the mental demand for all this atmosphere, and in it he shall enter. Let him refuse to admit dulness and depression, and they shall flee away as the shadows flee before the light. "The earth is full of the riches of the Lord." And man was formed in the divine image, and created that he might enter into and partake of all this infinite sweetness and exaltation. Let him rejoice and be glad forevermore.

> " Eat thou the bread which men refuse,
>   Flee from the goods which from thee flee,
>   Seek nothing, — Fortune seeketh thee."

The amount of pure exhilaration that is inherent in an obstacle and a difficulty has never been adequately estimated. There is really no such stimulus known elsewhere. It is like a ladder set up that one may climb. It is a tacit invitation to command the outlook. It is the open door of opportunity. It is the intimation to look within and discover one's latent powers and use them. It is one of the most forcible intimations of immortality.

Whether an obstacle shall be allowed to remain in its crude state as merely an obstacle, or whether it shall be transformed into a stepping stone — depends. It depends solely on

the amount of spiritual energy that can be
brought to bear. The amount of spiritual
energy that one can bring to bear on conditions depends on one's self, — on the way he
orders his physical and his spiritual life. And
as individual success and the world's progress
depend primarily on the manner in which man
conquers his difficulties, triumphs over the
obstacles in his path, on the way in which he
transforms and transfigures them by the
alembic of energy and melts them in the
crucible of exalted purpose, — as all the progress of the world depends primarily on this
power in the individual, it may not be amiss
to consider for a moment the conditions most
favorable to generating this all-potent and
irresistible energy.

Science as well as vision has recognized
that we dwell in an atmosphere of psychic
ether. Far more imponderable than air,
potent as magnetism, instant as electricity in
its action, it is the vast reservoir of power,
the source from which all may draw, and
whose force takes on the form of the indi-

vidual who draws upon it. To one, material activities and wealth; to another, learning; to another, means for benevolence; to another, artistic power, — to each, indeed, according to the laws of his demand. When Jesus said, "All power is given to me in heaven and in earth," it was merely the affirmation of his command over this infinite realm of psychic ether. He who can control this may command the very stones to become bread. And herein lies the very secret of life, wherein one may pluck out the heart of its mystery.

"If I regard iniquity in my heart the Lord will not hear me," says the Psalmist. Therein lies the key-note to the scale of power, — to free one's self from the weight of gloom and corrosive nature of iniquity, of all selfishness and self seeking, and possess, instead, the loadstone of right purpose. But as life is a complicated affair of physical as well as spiritual activity, the conditions for receiving the higher power must include both the bodily and the mental preparation.

It is not without significance that the prac-

tice of asceticism has made for so much among
a portion of mankind; not without significance
that " vegetarianism " and various other theories have held their sway and incited enthusiasm on the part of their followers. If
the body is the temple of the indwelling spirit,
it is the initial condition of the life of the
spirit that its temple be pure and lovely, and
fitting for its heavenly guest. Without making a fad or a fetish of any specific theory of
subsisting wholly on this, that, or the other, it
is yet true that the lightness and delicacy of
foods contribute infinitely more to both bodily
and spiritual energy than rich and heavy
viands. The connection between mind and
body is so close and so intimate that what
clogs the body burdens the mind. While perfect physical culture alone will never of itself
produce mental and spiritual energy, it is still
one of the essential conditions to its production. The physical culture of the day is for
the most part held not as a means to an end,
but as an end in itself; and so far as it is thus
viewed, it makes for little in the progress of

mankind. That a man should be an athlete
is of no importance; but if he achieve athletic
strength for the sake of applying that strength
to higher work, then by so much is he the
abler and the world the better for it.

When the conditions of daily life, however
full of charm and apparent prosperity they
have been, begin to crumble and recede, —
let them go. It is a sign of the new and the
untried. As well try to put the fruit or the
flower back into the seed, or the young bird
back into the egg, as to put back changing
conditions into their former scope and relation.
No matter how dear they have been, — how
indispensable they have seemed, — let them
go.

"Flee from the goods that from thee flee."

They have done their work for you and you
have done your work for them. Now cometh
the new. Go forward with faith, with abounding exhilaration, and its magnetism shall insure success. One might as well insist on
dwelling in the crumbling ruins and mouldy

cellars of the home of his ancestors, rather than go out into the life and light of a new home, as to insist on trying to revive old conditions that are evidently vanishing. Let them go. All that has been of worth in them is one's to hold in essence. It has entered into his character. The outer symbol vanishes and the inner significance remains.

> " A death-blow is a life-blow to some,
> Who, till they died, did not alive become;
> Who, had they lived, had died, but when
> They died, vitality began."

Seek nothing, for " Fortune seeketh thee." Seeking nothing, in the sense of anxious or worried questioning, let one yet hold himself receptive to all that is seeking him. There is the right niche for every human being; there is the one door which will open to him, and through whose portals he shall pass to the best possible conditions for his work and progress. Keeping himself in the true state of serene exhilaration and joy and confident belief, holding himself receptive to all

the infinite currents and tides of spiritual
forces, he shall find himself borne on to all
those conditions for his true advancement.
He shall taste the nectar and ambrosia of life.
Untold beauty and infinite charm shall attend
his way. The angels of the Lord shall en-
camp about him and shall bear him upward
and onward to the Wonderful Land.

*   *   *   *   *

Gaining an   The indulgence of a personal pref-
Outlook.   erence is usually an agreeable and
not infrequently a comparatively harmless
pastime; but there are undoubtedly occasions
in the life of every one where a preference
becomes a luxury, which, unless sacrificed, en-
forces and entails drudgery on some one else.
The world of progress moves on, indeed,
largely as the results of the work of men
and women who have learned how to sacrifice their preferences to the larger claim of
their duties.   There is very little earnest and
effective accomplishment whose very conditions of achievement do not lie in the sacrifice of certain tastes and inclinations, and it

is a great misfortune for a young person setting out in life to start from the point of view that he must never do anything except that which is agreeable to himself. The youth who believes himself, for instance, to be a poet, and thereby entitled to an honorary support by the community, rather than to be forced to turn his hand to those exceedingly commonplace but yet necessary occupations by which multitudes of people earn an honest living, is indulging his personal preferences at the expense of justice, not to say consideration, of other people. In applying for aid to what he may believe to be something not unlike a kindred world — to the world of scholars, poets, divines, persons, in short, who live by the earnings of intellectual activity, — the youth who declines to do anything disagreeable burdens people who, themselves, cheerfully and patiently undergo a vast amount of drudgery, and of things distasteful, every week of their lives. The statue is not carved, the pastoral work successfully administered, the novel created, the poem sung, without a very fair proportion of drudgery somewhere.

Dr. Holmes observes that he does not know of so easy a way of "shirking all the civic, and social, and domestic duties, as to settle it in one's mind that one is a poet;" and he continues: "I have therefore taken great pains to advise other persons laboring under the impression that they were gifted beings, destined to soar in the atmosphere of song above the vulgar realities of earth, not to neglect any homely duty under the influence of that impression. The number of these persons is so great, that if they were suffered to indulge their prejudice against every-day duties and labors, it would be a serious loss to the productive industry of the country."

There is a depth of truth in these words that may offer valuable food for meditation and suggest another outlook. The entire tendency must be transformed. He must learn the great lesson that the focus of success is within, not by rushing about and finding fault with other people ; not by laying the blame to circumstances or to this or that, but by centring all activity in right thought and right purpose, — at that moment and from that moment, — so will life proceed from a new point of departure on a higher plane. How often one sees a man expend sufficient force in recrimination and antagonism and general fault-finding with everybody and everything because he has lost some place or appointment that he held, — how often does he expend in this unworthy way force enough to have created for himself a dozen new places, each better than the one he has lost! In fact, the individual who meets change or disaster in a bitter and acrimonious spirit reveals by that very attitude that he was unfit for the office that he held. Let him sit down with himself and achieve harmony and concentration; let him generate psychic power sufficiently to act upon outward circumstances; and thus will he "reduce chaos to order and indraw the external to the centre." Then, indeed, will he have found his own central point, and find a basis from which to begin.

13

"Thought is the wages
For which I sell days."

No other wages are of value; for we do not
live in an atmosphere of negation, but of force.
When we do not receive this force it is because
we are, ourselves, impervious to it, and not
because the force is lacking. It can flow into
us only on certain conditions, of which harmony is the first requisite. The atmosphere
in which we live is as potent as electricity,
and all force in it is as infinite in supply as is
the air we breathe. One need not be tired, or
ill, or inactive if he but know how to draw on
this unlimited store. No one is living on that
ideal plane, on which it is perfectly possible to
live, until he learns to control circumstances
and conditions, and not be controlled by
them. The secret of this control lies in mental harmony. And its loss need never be
from any cause without, — the only danger
is within.

Dr. Anna Kingsford makes this significant observation on the deficiency of spiritual
vision : —

"The enemy of spiritual vision is always mate-rialism. It is, therefore, by the dematerialization of himself that man obtains the seeing eye and hearing ear in respect of Divine things. Demate-rialization consists not in the separation of the soul from the body, but in the purification of both soul and body from engrossment by the things of sense. It is but another example of the doctrine of correspondence."

The defect is always within; the remedy, too, is within. Nor is it a miracle. It is simply in adjusting himself to the conditions. Har-mony within works outward. "Out of the heart are the issues of life." One has only to keep love and faith and sweetness in his heart toward all, and circumstances and conditions will take care of themselves. It is the law and the prophets.

One comes into harmony thus by doing the duty of the hour, and doing it in the best manner possible. He must do it as unto the Lord. Life is ministry, and the thing in which one is engaged, whatever it may be, is for the time his means of entering into the general service. If his work is distasteful, to do it well is the surest way out of it into another that shall be more agreeable. For one should always make friends with even unfriendly conditions. Thus will he conquer them and emerge the more quickly. Disaster is often a form of initiation into a higher state; but if he rebels, the higher state is not possible, until he triumphs over all selfish feeling and comes into the beauty and largeness of harmony with the spiritual laws.

The soul is in bondage just as long as the eyes are closed to the larger significance and purpose of life. The moment this is perceived, all obstacles and miracles fall away of themselves. The man has wrought out his freedom. All the conditions that hamper us are of our own making; they will all dissolve like a dream the moment we achieve spiritual power, for " spirit is the positive; the event is the negative."

And the means lie in prayer; in the intense spiritual states generated by prayer. It is those which achieve and create conditions.

All circumstances on the invisible side are to be realized in the actual experiences of external life.

There are few words more significant than those of the apostle referring to Paul : " And the Lord said unto him, Arise, and go into the city, and it shall be told thee what thou must do." In a way, these words are typical of all life of the higher order. Every day the Voice says to us all, Arise ; go on, and it shall be told thee what to do. The secret of success is to banish anxiety about specific things, and only hold the intense longing for the good in whatever form it may come, — for the divine energy to flow in. It will cut its own channels and determine its own way. One need not be anxious about that.

One wants to be successful. But is he fitting himself for success by taking too anxious care over trifling details, or lamenting his privations or inconveniences ? The astral world around us is as much a fact as is the physical world, and all fret and discord is registered there and stamped in a way to react upon life.

It is in this way that the spirit, literally, builds
its own house. Mr. Sinnett, in an admirable
paper in the Nineteenth Century (entitled
" Behind the Scenes of Nature "), says of this
astral world : " The generally imperceptible
phenomena of the astral plane are, nevertheless, around us at every moment of our lives,
ready to brighten into objective existence for
persons who have developed certain interior
senses latent in every human being, though
cultivated as yet only among a comparative
few. The astral plane is a phase of nature
as extensive, as richly furnished, as densely
populous as the physical earth. It is, in one
sense, a counterpart presentment of that physical earth under different conditions. That
subtle medium in which the pictures of the
astral light are developed is plastic under the
influence of forces which do not, as a general
rule, control physical matter. To an extent
to which very few people in ordinary life have
any means of realizing, human thought is an
efficient agency in dealing with the matter of
the astral plane. Thoughts are things, and

according to the energy of the thought, the mind pictures are moulded into objective realities on the astral plane." And thoughts unite themselves (as they are good or evil, high or low) with corresponding forces on the astral plane. Spiritualization of the interior nature relates itself to spiritual forces on the other side of the physical world, and the person thus acquires that power of which Christ spoke when he declared that even greater things than He did, we should do.

Let one "arise and go into the city;" arise, and go into his own place of work, — to his desk, his easel, his shop, his office, with the feeling that his work is the Lord's, and that it shall be told him what to do. Let one feel that this day, this hour, are one step. It cannot last forever, even though it seem monotonous or hard. One may be creating, on the astral side, the new conditions into which he shall step, if he can but hold himself in harmonious receptivity to the tides of higher energy.

"Thought is all light;" and truth, indeed,

"has its roof and bed and board." Clinging
to truth, to light, to love, one is rich anywhere,
with a wealth that the world can neither give
nor take away. Thought is magnetic, and
brings in its train friends and forces.

*   *   *   *   *

Redemptive
Social
Agencies.

High above Hate I dwell;
O Storms! farewell.
Tho' at my sill your daggered thunders
    play
Lawless and loud to-morrow as to-day,
To me they sound more small
Than a young fay's foot-fall;
Soft and far sunken, forty fathoms low
In long ago,
And winnowed into silence on that wind
Which takes wars like a dust, and leaves but Love
    behind.
Hither Felicity
Doth climb to me,
And bank me in with turf and marjoram.
Such as bees lip, or the new-weaned lamb,
With tasselled barberry spines,
Bluets and columbines.
One grosbeak, too, 'mid apple buds a guest,
With bud-red breast,
Is singing, singing! All the hells that rage
Float less than April fog below our hermitage.

LOUISE IMOGEN GUINEY.

To dwell above hate is to open the doors to felicity. To dwell above strife is to dwell in the atmosphere of achievement. Humanity will only advance to its ultimate development of perfection in proportion as it rises above strife and passion and dwells in the serene air of harmonies.

There is a possible victory that awaits every human being because in each is the spark of the divine. We look about and recognize that this is peculiarly a time of dissension and of strife. Persons whose lives have been quiet and unofficial are suddenly dragged by circumstances into law suits and courts. The fierce light that traditionally beats upon a throne seems to beat upon each and every individual. It is a time of the working out of the karma, and the part of wisdom is to accept the current of events in a spirit of high and generous recognition and learn the lessons they have to offer. Old wrongs burn away in fierce fires; the old chapter is closed and a new one opens. It is a curious kind of judgment-day that prepares

the way for a new epoch. For the moment
the contemporary landscape seems to be one
where the majority are living the life of mate-
rialism ; living for bread alone : yet this is but
the most superficial view. In reality it is the
time when a new and deeper spirituality is
asserting itself.

The new conditions of life demand the
higher spirituality of the individual. But
what is this? Is it but a name, a mental
state of exaltation, an exhilaration, an ecstasy?
Is it a rhapsodic expression, an exalted hour,
or is it conduct? Is it a merely theoretical
thing, a vision caught in some rare hour of
silence and solitude? If it be thus it may
have a decorative value in ethics, but is de-
void of any practical bearing on our common
life. Unless spirituality is the power that
transforms falsehood to truth, selfishness to
generosity, meanness to magnanimity, unless
it enters into character as a pervasive force,
of what use can it be? Spirituality is not
negative. It is not the mere absence of sin.
It is the most positive state. It is the most
intense potency.

The present time is an adjustment of all general life. The panorama of the day reveals the working out of karma. It is the results that are left, and which form the material with which to inform the successive chapters of the future.

In all social relations hate and love operate as the two conflicting powers of good and evil. They are the two factors whose variations control all social life. Hardly less potent than the two primary factors is that variation of love we call friendship. No term holds a higher significance; no term is more misunderstood and misinterpreted. Many are the persons who imagine themselves to be good friends who do not know the meaning of the word. They are friendly to those who are friendly to them. They like persons who like them in return, and *vice versa.* Their plan of friendship is reciprocity. So much regard for so much regard in return. But is there not in this an unconscious selfishness, which is as real — even if on a more refined basis — as any selfishness of material life? Why not love

what is lovable, regardless as to whether one
is loved in return? Why not serve when
service is needed, regardless of whether it is
recognized or not? "He has always treated
you badly," remarks A to B of the absent C;
"apparently he has no regard for you, — why
should you put yourself out of the way for
him?"

Why? But why not? If C is in need of
a service that B can render, here is his privilege. Here is awaiting him one of the luxuries of life. The best gift heaven ever sends
is the power to be of service to our friends or
our foes, or to the stranger within our gates.
Whether this service is recognized or unrecognized does not matter. It is of no
conceivable consequence. This talk about
"gratitude" that is so much in the air is
disheartening. Does one render a service because, indeed, he desires to be paid in gratitude, and failing to receive this, would he
withhold or cancel the service? Ah, it is
Emerson, as usual, who points the truth. "If
you serve your friend because it is fit for you

to serve him," he says, "do not take back your
service when foolish people condemn you.
Adhere to your own act."

And beyond this is more. Let us grow out
of the sordid idea that because we do some
one a favor or render him a service, that he
is thereby under some transcendent obligation
to us. Let us recognize the truth — that it is
we who are obliged if he will permit us to
do him a favor. Why, to serve is gladness.
"He that is greatest among you let him be
your servant." To serve is a privilege; to *be*
served is not infrequently a penalty.

To dwell, then, in that serene upper air,
"high above Hate;" to dwell where Felicity
may come, thus it is to live in the atmosphere
of service and fidelity to friendships. Always
the poet's insight discerns the truth. It is
this for which the new conditions of life are
preparing us. The more one achieves spirituality the more he achieves happiness, — that
happiness that can only come when he dwells
"high above Hate."

It is not easy to account for the prevailing

idea that society is inherently sinful and solitude inherently saintly; that life in the social
world has a preponderance of vices, and that
the solitary life holds the balance of virtues,
and thus that brilliant, bewildering, fascinating thing we call society has its denouncers
as well as its devotees. But does the true
significance of life lie in solitude? Does it
not lie rather in those forces of active life
where character is tested and forged; where
criticism and comment and judgment, favorable or the reverse, meet and mingle; where
there is the strong stimulus of social magnetism? Solitude and society are not oppos-
ing, but complementary, forces; they are the
two sides of one experience, or the two experiences which mutually supplement and correct each other. The impulse of association,
to enter into the pleasure of the company of
others, — what is it but an impulse springing
from love and sympathy and interest? Surely,
it has its root in the diviner qualities.

The popular idea that society is heartless
and frivolous and hollow is not one to stand
the test of these higher questions.

"Here is a woman," says Phillips Brooks, "who says that society is responsible for her frivolousness; that no one can be purely earnest who lives in the midst of this fashionable world. But some other woman by her side confutes her, for she has shown how full social life may fill the character of what is best and sacredest."

Society — what is it, after all, but an aggregation of the one friend or companion? Instead of one, you meet many. Therefore it is the multiplication of opportunity, of privilege, of influence, of stimulus. If there is one place where selfishness and self-conceit and petty limitations of view and discordant feeling can be repressed and corrected, it is in the very heart of society. If there is any place in which all that is noble, true, generous, and beautiful can be fostered, it is there. These are the ideal possibilities of social intercourse.

The unerring register of its quality is the tone of its conversation. The privilege of meeting friends "with whom we may exchange a few reasonable words every day," as Emerson expresses it, is one of the choicest gifts of life. The term "companionship" is not infrequently limited to the relation existing between two persons alone; yet why should it not extend and multiply itself? Why should not society give companionship? And still we are all the time rich in the one and poor in the other. We encounter a vast amount of chatter to a very little conversation. Yet the moment that the individual—that all individuals—rise high enough in culture and in rich gifts of mind and heart, the aimless and empty chatter becomes impossible. For conversation is an expression of the entire individuality of the person, and it is high or low, according as he is high or low on intellectual and moral planes.

As things go, people meet all through a season in groups and parties and throngs — at teas, receptions, dinners, entertainments of all kinds — without exchanging a word in the way of genuine intercourse. But this is not the fault of society, but the defect in the individual. If he had anything of significance

to say he would probably say it. It is a
lack of intellectual purpose, of communicable
thought; and one curiously untrue conviction
growing out of this defective social intercourse is that it is a loss to give an hour to
one person alone, and that if one person is to
come it is as well to invite fifty and "clear
off" scores of social indebtedness. Where
inanities masquerade for ideas, society will be
dull or discordant, as may be. But elevate
and ennoble the individual, and it will be
brilliant and stimulating. It will key one up
to his best endeavors in life. It will call upon
him for his noblest energies. "True thought
and pure love are immortal," says Bishop
Spalding, "and whatever opinions as to other
things a man may hold, all know that to be
human is to be intelligent and moral. . . . He
who believes in culture must believe in God;
for what but God do we mean when we talk
of loving the best thoughts and the highest
beauty? If he believe that God is infinite
power working for truth and love . . . then
he is certain of himself, and feels no fear or

14

anger when his opinions are opposed. He
learns to bear what he cannot prevent, knowing that courage and patience make tolerable
irremediable ills." Here is the true ideal of
social intercourse; the fidelity to spiritual
standards of life and the infinite toleration
of infinite love. Let one go "into society"
with "a meek and lowly heart, a free and
illumined mind, and a soul without fear."
The best gifts of life are our friends and our
opportunities, Mr. Depew has said; society is
the union of both. Social intercourse offers
the most valuable opportunities — it is the
door to all combination and achievement;
and opportunities offer friends and each multiplies the other.

There is something in holding all social
relations as a fine art and developing them
to finer issues. To recognize in each ac-
quaintance or friend his ideal self, which is
the vision of his possibilities, is to call on
him to realize these in word and deed. This
idealizing regard is the most potent stimulus
to all that is worthy. It is something to take

out into the social atmosphere as factors of
the finer civilization that will result from
the higher individual life. The man who feels
that he is trusted will never betray the trust.
The individual who feels that his larger possibilities are recognized and appreciated will
live from this nobler plane. Thus society in
general has its responsibility to the individual
just as truly as the individual has to society.
And it is in the heart of life, in the storm or
stress, that one must live the life and not
merely talk the talk. The higher qualities
of life must be dramatized into active service,
and thus does one think the best thoughts
and love the highest beauty.

And the field is the world. To live the life
of the spirit in the midst of its turmoil is the
hardest test; yet it is only the spiritual coward
who runs away.

> " Tho' there come a million,
> Wise Saadi dwells alone."

But it is a question as to whether Saadi is
wise when he prefers to dwell alone. Living

on earth, is it not one's duty to hear many
voices that ring in its air? Is one's life for
mere acquirement, or to show results and
flower into influence and deed?

There is but one answer. The sociologists
have an expression for a certain kind of culture which is the art of living well with one's
kind. Education, too, as a science recognizes
this; and one of the chief values in the kindergarten is to accustom the child to the companionship of his fellows, to teach him the
art of living well with them. In this ideal
system all the higher nature of the child is
cultivated. He learns justice and generosity,
sacrifice and consideration. It is the culture
of the divine nature in him, overmastering
mere physical instincts or propensities which
are animal and not spiritual in their nature.
The little "gifts" of the kindergarten system
all further this fine culture, and the entire race
would be largely redeemed if every child received first this beautiful training.

The principle prevails in after life. To live
well with one's kind, — in its full sense this
includes almost the entire art of life.

The trend of civilization gives added emphasis to this. Co-operative living in some form is largely on the increase. For what are all hotel and hotel apartment and apartment house living — what are they all but forms of co-operation ? Instead of one house to one family, there is one house to a dozen or a hundred families. The best city hotels are largely filled in the winter with resident guests who have been householders, whose furniture is very likely stored in warehouses, with the vague idea that sometime it may be wanted again, while meantime they take a suite of rooms, take meals in the large dining-room common to all the guests, rely on the general service of the house instead of having private service, and in the dining-room common to all, the elevator, the corridors, meet and mingle continually. The enforced society may go no farther; but certainly people cannot live under a common roof for years, in the incidental daily meeting, without having it largely in their power to contribute to their neighbor's comfort, or to detract from it. In

the apartment-hotel and apartment-house living the contact is less; yet in the apartment
hotel the guests are apt to share a common
dining-room. In the apartment house they
share the entrance and the elevator, at least.
In all city, town, and village life, social contact, even aside from social occasions, is the
continual rule. The churches, the theatres,
the concert halls, the shops, the cars, the side-
walks — are all shared. When one contemplates all these perpetual opportunities to meet
and mingle; an enforced association that no
one can escape; the privileges or the penal-
ties that result from it, one is almost ready to
concede that the art of living well with one's
kind is the divinest of the arts. Certainly, if
one study the teachings of the Master he will
see what supreme importance the Christ laid
on the means and measures necessary to live
well with one's kind. "Judge not, that ye be
not judged." "Love is the fulfilling of the
law." "Do unto others as ye would that they
should do unto you."

One need not multiply the texts. They

would fill pages, and each knows them for
himself. They are all summed up in the
command, — " *Love* one another." " He that
loveth his brother abideth in the light, and
there is no occasion of stumbling in him."

If one thinks of it, there would seem to be a
close connection between the command not to
judge and to love. Harsh judgments, unjust
judgments, are at the root of nine-tenths of all
social friction. A harsh and an unjust judgment are almost synonymous. A harsh judgment is almost invariably both an ignorant
and an unjust one. Wider knowledge is
tolerance. Finer insight is sympathy. Large
comprehension is love.

The harsh judgment, even if unspoken, instantly begins its corrosive work. Let one
think evil of another, and though he shall
never utter it, never write it, in no way make
it audible or visible, the object of this thought
will feel it, and friction between the two will
begin. On the contrary, let one hold another
in perpetually beautiful thought, let him refuse
to recognize any evil, and call on him — spirit

to spirit — only for the good, and this silent, subtle thought will so invigorate and stimulate all the ideal nature of its object that the man will grow to really be that which his neighbor believes him to be. Now to so live is not only a beautiful, an ideal state ; it is not only a privilege, it is a duty — the highest duty. It is the absolute divine responsibility on each and all.

To live well with one's kind includes in its higher possibilities this holding of sweet and helpful and believing thought of every one. It does not matter that the person may *seem* rude, selfish, censorious, or ill-bred. Hold him all the more in the higher thought. The trend of life, all advance f civilization, is more and more toward intimate social contact. The times demand development in the art of living well with one's kind. Solitude is all-essential for receiving divine light and direction. Society is essential for carrying that illumination out into life and transmuting it into influence.

Life is, after all,— this present life, — to learn

to live, to learn to live the life of the spirit, which asserts its force over our physical states, and which transforms all lower feeling into love, joy, peace, and holiness.

Let the days be steeped in color and perfume and music and loveliness; let them glow with all the fire of the opal, and reflect in their many-faceted hours a thousand charms and visions of beauty. Redeem time from cold and narrow calculations, and set it free to be lived with romance and ardor and imaginative intensity. Let it radiate joy, and let the basis of reality be glorified by the superstructure of romance in sympathies, and swift, unerring intuition. While living, let us *live*, not exist. If one will but turn toward Beauty, her magnetic tides shall set toward him, and his days shall be steeped in ecstasy, and all the divine glory of Beauty and Love.

THE UNSEEN WORLD.

The other world is not another place, but another
view. — KANT.

Death occurs when certain relations in the organism are not adjusted to the relations in the environment. — HERBERT SPENCER.

> Afraid? Of whom am I afraid?
>
> . . . . .
>
> Of resurrection? Is the East
> Afraid to trust the morn
> With her fastidious forehead?
> As soon impeach my crown! — EMILY DICKINSON.

Those who know Christ are sensibly co-ordinated
with the spiritual world and penetrated by its life. —
PROF. JOHN H. DENISON, in "Christ's Idea of the
Supernatural."

If we could only know, somewhat as John must have
known after his vision, the presence of God into
which our friend enters on the other side, the higher
standards, the larger fellowship with all his race, and
the new assurance of personal immortality in God; if
we could know all this, how all else would give way to
something almost like a burst of triumph as the soul
which we loved went forth to such vast enlargement,
to such glorious consummation of its life. — PHILLIPS
BROOKS.

THE INCIDENT OF DEATH.

The rose we gathered not
　　Blooms in the soul forever,
And hands ne'er joined in life
　　Death has no power to sever.
　　　　　　　LILLA CABOT PERRY.

Glory to God! to God! he saith,
Knowledge by suffering entereth
And life is perfected by Death.
　　　　　　　TENNYSON.

Lord! how in darkness can I see aright?
Child! all the universe I fill with light;
Be true within, and truth shall cleanse thy sight.

More than all speech the Silent Order saith,
All laws of life are articles of faith;
Who loves and seeks for good, behold he prayeth.
　　　　　　　CHARLES GORDON AMES.

O think of death, to hold ideas or views or beliefs about it, is simply to hold views, ideas, or beliefs about life. The first great idea, perhaps, that we want to hold deeply is that death is not

the *end* of life but simply an event *in* life.
The life itself goes on under new conditions just
as life goes on in another country when a man
leaves his home in one place or in one country
to create a new one in another State or country. The youth who leaves New England and
goes to the Pacific Coast to live is not, as a
man of fifty, the same person who, thirty
years before, left his home ; nor is he probably
the same person he would have been had he
passed his entire fifty years of life in his native
town ; yet his identity remains unchanged, his
essential life has gone on. He did not leave
his life behind him when he changed his
State, or his country. Does not this analogy
hold true in regard to the changed conditions
in which the man lives after the event called
death ?

That persistence of energy which we call
life is spirit. Spirit is immortal ; its life,
eternal. The physical body it inhabits is
neither immortal nor eternal. It is simply the
temporary tenement of the spirit. To keep it
pure, refined, healthful, is a part of spiritual

life; for it is the means through which the higher life must express itself. But it is *not* that higher life in itself, only the instrument. The spiritual is rooted in the natural. "That is not first which is spiritual, but that which is natural," says St. Paul. Dr. Drummond makes the truth very clear when he says: "The spiritual world is simply the outermost segment, circle or circles of the natural world. For purposes of convenience we separate the two just as we separate the animal world from the plant. But the animal world and the plant world are the same world. They are different parts of one environment. And the natural and spiritual are likewise one. The inner circles are called the natural, the outer the spiritual. And we call them spiritual simply because they are beyond us or beyond a part of us. What we have correspondence with we call natural; what we have little or no correspondence with we call spiritual. But when the organism freely communicates with these outer circles the distinction necessarily disappears. The spiritual to it becomes the outer circle of the natural."

Now to just that degree in which a man dwelling in the natural world corresponds with the spiritual, in just that degree is he alive ; the more entirely he is a part of the spiritual world the more is he alive. "To be carnally minded is death, but to be spiritually minded is life and peace." There is the condensation of the truth regarding both lives ; to live merely the physical life of eating and sleeping and personal, selfish pleasure and indulgence, is death. To live that life to which food and sleep and personal pleasures or indulgences are means to an end, and that end the service of humanity, the achievement of a higher purpose, that is to be alive. The event of death does not transform the individual, as by a miracle, into spirituality. The tendency toward the spiritual must be greater by leaving the natural environment; but spirituality is a growth. Many a man still in the physical body is on a higher spiritual plane, and may live more entirely the spiritual life, than one who has left the body. All depends on the quality of the spirit, — as to how great a degree it has come into correspondence, or communion with the divine.

Kant says that the other world is not another place, but another view. This undoubtedly defines for us the nature of the first immediate experiences after the event of death. The spiritual body, — which is the perfect body, after whose form the physical body is fashioned, — released from its outer case or tenement, finds itself in a new world that is yet the old world, only it has gained the "other view." It has added powers. It can move swiftly and at will; it has infinitely greater capacities and powers. It is now adapted to a higher plane; it corresponds to a more spiritual environment. Undoubtedly the clearer vision and finer perception of those who have passed the event of death behold the panorama of this world as we behold that of the animal or the vegetable world. They are to be seen and heard and felt equally by us if our preceptions

15

are equal to it. The spiritual world is not invisible to the natural by reason of any space or limits, but only through conditions. As man achieves spirituality he comes into proportionately clearer and larger recognition and perception of all spiritual life and form.

To just that degree in which now and here we live the spiritual life do we deal with spiritual forces. Anything that a man desires to do he will be enabled to achieve if his purpose is unselfish and noble and he live on this spiritual plane. There is no extravagance, but literal truth, in Emerson's assertion : "If a god wishes to ride, every chip and stone will bud and shoot out wingèd feet to carry him." In the realm of spirit our finer and more intense forces work. These may be used by all who are in correspondence with this environment.

And all this is simply an interpretation in other words of the essential faith of the Christian Church. The only achievement of spirituality lies in nearness to God. The gateway of this higher life is prayer. This life of the spirit is man's normal life; it is his destiny. "The whole secret of the physical has not been read until its power of becoming spiritual, by service of the spirit, has been read."

The time has come even now when man must abandon worldliness and live as a soul; when the City of God must not be thought of as only to be entered after death, but that it is the responsibility of every man to create it now and here.

It is no extravagance to say that this work of making heaven on earth is the real business of every human being. All else is incidental, and should lead up to this supreme aim. "A great integrity makes us immortal," and so we may, and should be, immortal now. We "live by will, by thought, by virtue," and "we die by sloth, by disobedience." Some persons are much more alive, much more immortal than others; but it is a matter of achievement and not of endowment.

In whatever degree one will place himself in the currents of spiritual receptivity he shall receive of the heavenly magnetism.

There is, perhaps, no greater barrier to living the higher life, now and here, than the traditional idea of going to heaven after the change called death. It is spoken of as a definite thing, like "going to" Europe after the voyage. But that spiritual state of harmony and holiness which we call heaven must be begun this side of death, to be continued on the other. It is an achievement, not an attainment. It must be created, not found. To live in heaven after we die we must live in heaven before we die.

Nor are there wanting those who realize this, — beautiful and noble and angelic souls all around us, who live the heavenly life here on earth and offer us the visible pledge and prophecy of immortality, — who live, even while here on earth, —

" In pulses stirred to generosity,
 In deeds of daring rectitude, in scorn
 For miserable aims that end with self,
 In thoughts sublime that pierce the night like stars,
 And with their mild persistence urge man's search
 To vaster issues "

The earnest and sympathetic student of human nature will, indeed, find more of the divine .in each and every one than on mere superficial knowledge he would have believed. Humanity is not worse, but rather better, than it is invariably held to be.

*   *   *   *   *

Nourished in Miracles. "Born and nourished in miracles,
His feet were shod with golden bells."

This world is a miracle world, and time slips by invested in a series of fascinating interests. The new discoveries in science lead one to stand breathless before the won-der-workings of electricity, and of a new force which is greater even than that, and is even the law that holds the stars in their courses. The demands of the age for writing transcend the powers of the hand and the pen, and the typewriter appears. Again, the demands transcend individual powers, and the need is for some invention so subtle and so marvel-lous that it will transmit the thought in the mind to the paper without the intervention

of the hand. That invention is already taking shape. The telegraph, too, promises to
take the burden of correspondence and do
away with letters by mail. A means still
more subtle, more swift, more remarkable,
dawns among the possibilities in the law of
suggestion.

At a meeting of the Society for Psychical
Research recently, a paper was read narrat-
ing many most interesting instances of the
cure or the prevention of pain by means of
silent suggestion by the practitioner to the
mind of the patient that no pain should be
felt. To one who intended the next day to
visit a dentist, it was suggested that during
those hours no pain should be felt. No pain
was felt in the dental operations. Numerous
and varied incidents were related, all of exceeding interest, and leading to unexplored
fields of speculation. It is probable that the
form of mental cure that denies the reality of
pain at all works on this same law, suggesting
to the subjective or subliminal self that it
shall rejoice in wholeness and energy, and

that it has no illness or pain. Going back far enough we find Dr. Quimby, a half century or so ago, in Portland, Me., using a form of suggestion, the story of which has been most interestingly told in a book by Mrs. Dresser. Many — perhaps most — people will find by experimenting that they are susceptible to auto-suggestion, and that they can prevent or diminish or cure pain and suffering, as may be, by this power. To suggest to one's self, as he is falling asleep, that he is to awaken at a certain hour, is, almost invariably, to waken at the precise time. To suggest to one's self, just as he is falling asleep, that he will rise with unusual energy and radiance and power of accomplishment in the morning, is, largely, to gain an increase of force that is almost astounding. In like manner, one can suggest to a friend to come and see him ; to the absent, to write a letter ; indeed, there is no limit to the use that may be made of this power.

In any case of estrangement, or of misun-understanding, this law of suggestion is often far better than are verbal explanations, or discussion, or any interchange of letters. It does not differ from that method designated by many occultists as putting a certain thing "into the silence." Practically it is the same thing. If a friend is estranged, think good thoughts to him. Suggest to him in this telepathic way that everything is right; that there is harmony, not discord; and nine times out of ten harmony will result.

It is not just to consider this subject without referring it to the best book ever written upon it, — one that is an efficient hand-book of the inner life, — Mr. Henry Wood's "Ideal Suggestion." In this, a number of years ago, Mr. Wood formulated the law and presented it in the most clear, simple, and impressive way. Suggestion and auto-suggestion offer the most potent means for the prevention and cure of physical disease, for moral regeneration, for intellectual energy, for spiritual achievement. Let a writer try the experiment of suggesting to himself that at a certain hour on a certain day he will write a story,

a poem, an essay. When the time comes he
will, if susceptible to auto-suggestion, do precisely this thing. The artist will find in it his
supreme stimulus. The auto-suggestion will,
in some mysterious way, set in train the forces
that produce the result.

The key to the phenomena of auto-suggestion, or of suggestion, lies in the truth asserted
by that learned man and great, metaphysician,
Professor Bierregaard of New York, who says:
"The real man lives in another world." The
real man is the spiritual being who is the
tenant of the body, but whose essential life
is on a higher plane than that on which the
conscious life is lived. This spiritual being,
the higher self, has powers infinitely above
those of which he is conscious: it has vision
to behold what the natural eyes cannot
see; its scope in all ways transcends the
natural life. When this being suggests to
the lower or conscious self, execution and
accomplishment follow. The key to all greatness of life lies in living this life of the
spirit.

There is probably just as much communication taking place all the time on the subliminal plane, between all persons, as there is on the natural and visible plane, — in a manner, too, far more direct and personal.

"Star to star vibrates light; can soul to soul
  Strike through a finer element than its own?"

Most certainly it can; most certainly it does. Emerson speaks of our friendships as "hurrying to poor and lame conclusions." They do, — a large proportion of them, — and the reason lies in their being too personal, too much a thing of visible and tangible contact, and too little a mutual spiritual attitude. If a friendship cannot inspire faith without constant letters or constant visits, it is neither worth the having nor the holding. Its significance is in proportion to its spirituality. Any real relation grows greater and more exalted by being held on a plane above the merely personal. Suggestion plays in it the most potent part. For this is a miracle world in which we are living, and a new set of powers, an

entirely new range of activities, are dawning upon our vision.

The divinity within cannot assume its true place as the controller of life, the creator of circumstance, until it is fully recognized. "If we think seriously on the matter, it is not difficult to understand that the physical body with the passions and desires does not constitute the real man ; for we know it is possible to train, control, and use them. This implies an actor above or behind the physical body to whom the latter is an instrument. It is more difficult to realize that the mind is also an instrument, and that it is not the mind itself which controls the body, but that the real man stands even back of the mind, and uses it and can train it for greater and greater use as an instrument. The mind is an instrument by means of which man may control his lower external nature."

An essential truth that should be held as the basis of all living is that we are each responsible for the quality and the direction of our life; that there is no excuse for living

from lower motives, and that, when we eliminate envy, selfishness, all forms of self seeking,
we also eliminate most, if not all, of the tendencies that drag us downward to low per-
formance and to unhappiness. Let one steep
his consciousness in the one great impulse to
give and not to get; to radiate truth, energy,
sunny stimulus as he goes on his daily way, —
not merely to his friends, his associates, his
companions, but to all with whom he is in-
cidentally or accidentally in contact, — and at
once the whole face of creation is changed to
him.

One. contemplates, we will say, a change to
another locality, and he begins to concern
himself with speculations or anxieties regarding what may accrue to him there in riches,
consideration, fortune. But let him reverse
this train of thought. Let him forget himself, and think only of the manner in which
he may live his life; in which he may enter
into large and sympathetic relations with
others, and give of the best his soul has
received. Instantly, then, does anxiety van-

ish, and peace and energy and new stimulus take possession of him. He may believe and go forward.

To refer one's consciousness to this higher nature is to create the conditions through which it may work. The entire direction of life should be committed to this essential self. The lower nature has its lower inclinations, its tendencies to all manner of unworthy thoughts and inadequate aims. But this need not matter. They can all be controlled. "I beseech you," said St. Paul, "that you walk not after the flesh but after the spirit." What does he mean but that the higher being within us should take command of the mind and of the body? should deny selfish desires, idle aims, and frivolous tendencies? should resolutely close the portals against unworthy phases of thought? This it is to walk after the spirit.

It is a question if genius — that inscrutable mystery, is more than this, — to come into conscious and close communion with the higher, the essential self. The soul or this

higher self has garnered light, wisdom, and is
capable of illuminating the whole being.   But
there are conditions that must be observed.
The kingdom of heaven is truly within, and it
is the secret of success to find it.   Here is the
clear vision that perceives the inner truth, the
just relations of all things.   If the mind can
but effect the union and identify itself with
this higher being which is the real man, then
can it direct its path and move onward in the
way of all nobleness.   Browning recognizes
this higher self when he makes Paracelsus
say : —

> " Truth is within ourselves ; it takes no rise
>   From outward things, whate'er you may believe ;
>   There is an inmost centre in us all
>   Where truth abides in fulness."

This higher self lives, not in the earthly, but
in the heavenly world.   There is its home, its
native atmosphere.   There does it receive of
eternal wisdom ; and by keeping the mind and
heart in the pure atmosphere of love and
aspiration this wisdom may be constantly com-
municated and guide the lower life.   " Per-

sonal aspiration" is personal responsibility.
The thing one longs for one can achieve. The
very fact of the longing is proof and prophecy. One has no right to disregard his aspirations. They are the truest part of his life.
They are the messages from his essential self.
They are the indications and the direction of
his life. One's primary business in this world
is to realize his aspirations. All great men
have applied themselves to this one work, —
through toil and hardship it might be and it
usually has been, but that matters not. That
is merely the incidental scenery along the way.
Always is it true that "The height your hope
hath found your feet may reach."

The Law of Suggestion, as set forth by
Liébault, offers what is fairly a key to life,
and one by which those who learn to use it
aright may transform their entire scheme of
existence.

For, if this subjective mind is a kind of
reservoir into which infinite currents flow, and
if the quality and quantity of it that we may
draw, daily and hourly, depend on the sug-

gestion to it from the conscious mind, it is evident that we thus have control over the entire psychic force that goes to dominate our lives. By reinforcing the mental power with learning, with earnest purpose, with moral zeal, we suggest to this infinite reservoir of the objective the quality of power we expect it to send forth.

It is this power of suggestion that is probably at the basis of what is known as mental healing, or the metaphysical cure. The imagination, the power of realizing mental images, has a direct and a powerful effect on the brain, and this dominates the vitality. If the influence can be made powerful enough the cure is effected, and the result is in proportion to the strength of conviction and to the force of the impression received by the imagination. Nor is there anything unreal about this. Nothing is so real as imaginative impressions; nothing is so abiding and so all-determining as these. In illness of a nervous character the mental cure is almost sure to be a success, and its results are as swift as they are sure.

Now if the power of suggestion is so marvellous on the physical side of life, is it not equally so on the moral or the mental? Cannot a higher degree of perfection in various directions be suggested, and will not such suggestions prove seed thoughts, that will germinate and grow and exalt and transform character? Or cannot the beauty of life be thus suggested — the charm of a day? Can it not be said, — cannot one say to one's self in the early morning, before his solitude has yet been broken, — This day shall be one of enchantment and loveliness? It is to be peopled with noble and beautiful presences; in it I shall meet friends with whom I stand in real relations, although they may be as yet unknown to me; they are to be the friends and associates of my future, and in their inspiring companionship I shall rise to new heights of life and thought and endeavor. This day, too, shall be consecrated by beautiful thoughts. Into it shall enter nothing unworthy. I shall walk hand in hand with my ideal of life, and realize, in outward experience, my aspirations.

16

It will be a day of inspiration, a day in which
all gladness of the heavenly radiance shall
shine. It is to be lived on the spiritual plane
on which alone is our real life, and not on the
lower and material.

The experiment is one easily tried, and it is
really one worth trying. It is very curious to
see the results that sometimes follow it, — the
sudden appearance of charming people, heretofore unknown, or delightful letters or events
equally unexpected.

It is perfectly possible from this uplifting of
the soul and this power of serious mental suggestion to thus magnetize the conditions of
a day in the early morning on awakening, and
transform all its scenery and all its events, till
one lives, indeed, in a world beautiful, and
sees life as from the Mount of Transfiguration.

     *   *   *   *   *

The Cloud of Witnesses. A writer of undoubted authority
recently gave the following as hav-
ing been written for him, automati-
cally, by an intelligence professing to be from
the spiritual world : —

"We live a full, active life without an earth or material body, as you understand that term.

"We are endowed in our natures with immortal life, and we shall never cease to be.

"We are subject to general laws, universal of application to all in this earth spirit sphere.

"Disobedience or inattention to these laws dwarfs the powers of the soul, and relegates it to a lower sphere, where it must seek through the law which it violated in thought or purpose its restoration and advancement, or sink still deeper into the darkness which comes of its own neglect or misdeeds.

"There is no known limit to acquirement, either of knowledge or personal grace. We, ourselves, cannot understand the meaning of infinity in its fulness. It is because we, like yourselves in the mortal, are finite.

"The highway between our sphere and your earth is open, and we who desire your good or happiness are permitted to travel it when we will.

"We can impress you, and will yet make more palpable disclosures of ourselves to you when you obey the laws of your spiritual being, and place yourself *en rapport* with us, bidding us welcome."

Such communication, if from the subjective mind rather than from an intelligence outside

this life, offers food for very interesting speculation. That potent and unrecognized law of
nature, vibration, is making itself felt in the
world of thought and perception, as electricity,
in its new and larger applications, is impressing
itself as the supreme force in all the applied
arts. This law is giving to us daily and hourly
perception of unseen presences with us, — of
the cloud of witnesses. Science has long since
recognized vibration in the physical world.
The imponderable power which at one rate of
vibration was heat, at another light, illustra-
ting in its various phases the beautiful law of
the correlation of forces, has been recognized;
and on the corresponding spiritual side this
law holds just as it does in the natural world.
The law in both its aspects, natural and spiritual, is as old as creation, — as is electric force,
although it has required nearly nineteen hundred years to begin to find out how to use
electricity to the best service of man. So
likewise is it only beginning to dawn upon the
mind that in vibration lies the secret of many
wonderful things. The explanation of the

phenomena of unconscious cerebration lies undoubtedly in the law of vibration. As man is essentially a spiritual being, his spiritual self has those powers of hearing and seeing which to the physical self seem to reside in the eye and the ear. But the physical sight and hearing are limited to the smallest extent, while the spiritual sight and hearing are on an altogether different scale.

The spiritual hearing is sensitive to vibrations; it undoubtedly takes cognizance of things outside the limits of the physical ear, and under certain conditions it reports these to the lower consciousness, and thus occurs the phenomena of unconscious cerebration. The spiritual hearing may be aware of words spoken across a hemisphere; the spiritual sight may perceive experiments made, or ideas recorded, or a thousand things that occur which the normal sight cannot perceive; this higher consciousness, which is always more or less in touch with the universal, receives knowledge and thought in ways wholly outside the ordinary methods of acquiring knowledge.

Here is this inmost centre "where truth abides in fulness;" here is the true message to be found; the true voice to which to listen. The higher spiritual round on which the race stands to-day enables many to perceive the reality of the law of vibration, and to trace to it results whose cause has before been conjectural. The words spoken in a room are photographed, as it were, on the air, and can be read afterward by one whose perceptions are sufficiently developed. The "atmosphere" of a room, in its spiritual sense, is as much a fact as in the quality of air. Personal friendships may be made or broken by words spoken which, outwardly, the object of them never hears, but whose vibration penetrates to his spiritual understanding. This has always been true regarding certain exceptional natures; but with the great spiritual impetus now so widely felt there are a largely increasing class of people whose perceptions are open to the subtle messages that flash through space by the law of vibration.

The expression, "entering the silence," is

simply entering the atmosphere of vibrations. Here the eye and the ear that is developed to this fine ether sees visions and hears messages which convey the deepest truth. Here all the degrees of personal regard and love and friendship are strengthened or are weakened and broken.

Nothing in earth or heaven is more significant than love and friendship. A life without these, if one could conceive of it, were barren, indeed, even though it need not be despondent or fruitless, if it be loyal to its own high purposes. But loves and friendships must come of themselves; they must be a matter of spiritual gravitation; they cannot be commanded or entreated. Nor can one command or entreat himself in giving regard beyond that of the good will and cordial sweetness which is the natural and spontaneous overflow of sweetness of spirit. Any regard beyond this of special friendship or love must be spontaneous, must give itself, one knows not why, or not be given at all. To entreat special friendship is useless, for it

cannot be produced at will. Our friendships
are our magnetisms. It is quite possible they
do not always flow toward the worthiest
in all respects, but they do flow naturally, in
the channels of sympathetic companionship
and mutual tastes and interests. Intellectual
and artistic sympathies are a stronger bond
than the merely emotional qualities. Culture,
in all its fine significance, is the strongest of
mutual ties among friends; the culture that
responds easily and naturally to all the world
of thought, and art, and literature, and social
life. Friendship and love, in the sense of
good will, are easily given; in the sense of
companionships, of those we choose to be
the sharers of our social life, it is quite a different matter. In that must the element of
mutual sympathy, in the intellectual and artistic world, be the determining quality. To
give love in the sense of good will is a part
of the higher life; to give the intimacy of
personal companionships is predetermined by
range of temperamental affinities over which
one has no immediate control. These are mu-

tually harmonious or discordant — according to vibrations of the spiritual currents.

Thought transference is explained by the law of vibration. As electricity can be conducted through the air without a wire, so thought, vibrating through space from one mind to another, carries distinct impressions and recognized messages. All social life is just as much determined by our attitude toward a friend in his absence as it is in his presence. The inner thought and the feeling toward him reach him by means of the law of vibration.

" Mind is designed for mastery," well says a recent writer on psychic development. " The psychic vibrations of focalized desire upon the inner medium of communication — the spiritual ether — create the light in which the object of desire is perceived ; hence the clearness of vision depends upon the completeness of inward focalization." This truth is as applicable in perceiving and creating external states and conditions of life as it is in perceiving objects or persons at a distance. It is simply the essential self that asserts its supremacy, and by psychic concentration produces a scale of vibrations that create new sets of achievements, new conditions, new environment.

The growth and development of higher faculties will inevitably enlarge and extend all life. The world is one thing to the savage and quite another to the man of education and culture. It is one thing to the rudimentary powers and another to him whose powers are developed. The powers that assert themselves as faculties of mind in the higher life are faith, hope, and love. It is in the growth of these that humanity comes toward perfection. By living in these faculties the vital centre is transferred from the physical to the spiritual. So far as a man's nature becomes spiritualized, so far does it become one of power to dominate and transcend all conditions.

That period of the world's history has evidently come when the barriers between this part of life and the part entered upon after the event we call death have grown almost transparent. The two worlds — that of the spiritual and the physical — are coming into recognized relation. The change is as great and as definite as was that established between the Eastern and the Western Continents by the laying of the submarine cable. Not only is there coming to be more direct and recognizable communication between the seen and the unseen, but the same phenomenon is repeated between mind and mind, spirit and spirit, in the world of the seen. Thought transference is rapidly attaining the exactness of science. The observations are being reduced to data, and out of the data shall the law be formulated.

Happiness comes in proportion to the freedom, and responsiveness of the higher nature. In this more magnetic and intense and responsive atmosphere lie undreamed-of possibilities of beauty and happiness. One has but to turn to the light and live. One will find each morning this marvellous power in his hands to rise in newness of life and to shape conditions for the day. The hours

lie before him like plastic clay, ready to take
the impress of his spiritual design. Let one
stamp them with the force of aspiration, the
design of generous purpose. Let him resolve
that the day shall be lived "as unto the
Lord;" that it shall be conducted to its close
in serene dignity, fair faith, and loving belief;
that it shall be lived in the beauty of holiness.
These words have been to us a kind of rhetorical phrasing; but let one think of them for a
moment. The *beauty* of holiness. Not merely
the ethics of holiness, but the beauty of it, —
as the highest expression of loveliness. Gaining this, shall the Lord preserve thy going out
and thy coming in, — the Lord shall preserve
thee from all evil forevermore!

*   *   *   *   *

**With What
Body Do
They Come?**

And verily many thinkers of the age,
Aye, many Christian teachers, half in
   heaven,
Are wrong in just my sense who under-
   stood
Our natural world too insularly, as if
No spiritual counterpart completed it;
Consummating its meaning, rounding all

To justice and perfection, line by line,
Form by form, nothing single nor alone,
The great below clenched by the great above.
— *Aurora Leigh.*

It cannot be denied that the supreme event in life is death. It marks the greatest definite crisis. It is the withdrawal of the individual from his visible and tangible relations with the visible and tangible world. It is the process by which he emerges from the physical body and is clothed in his spiritual body. Death is not, of course, the *end* of life, but an event *in* life which closes one phase of its experience. It is sacred but not sad. It has the profoundest speculative interest as well as the deepest spiritual significance.

There are, however, many events in the course of a lifetime which mark as definite epochs the greatest event of death. "Men talk of another life beyond the grave," said the Princess Halm-Eberstein to her son, Daniel Deronda; "I have long since entered on another life." Most people who live intensely, experience this feeling. The youth

who goes from the quiet uneventfulness of
a country life into the activities of the city,
may well feel, after a period of years, that
he has entered on "another life." Sometimes the experiences that might be diffused
through a dozen lifetimes seem to concen-
trate themselves, in successive periods, in one.
We see a life composed of as many "states"
as the productions of a great artist. It has its
"movements," like the onward, majestic sweep
of a symphony.

> "Out of the quiet ways,
> Into the world's broad track,
> We go forth, in the summer days,
> And never wander back.
>
> Not death!
> We do not call it so;
> Yet scarcely more with dying breath
> Do we forego."

Kant tells us that "the other world is not
simply another place, but another view," and
we are all by way of having a number of
"other worlds" in this one in which we are
now living.

What a different world is Boston, for instance, to Edward Everett Hale from what it
is to the criminal, the drunkard! Each may
walk the same street, but how different the
world the one is living in from the other!
The great archæologist goes to Rome or to
Egypt. He finds, in the same place, a different world from that which the ordinary tourist
recognizes. The poet, the philosopher, has
each his own world. So those who have
passed through that event we call death may
find their sphere of action among us, working
in co-operation with us just in proportion as
we live spiritually enough to co-operate with
higher spiritual forces than our own. If we
could but realize the divine loveliness of all
this interweaving of the natural and spiritual
life, all gloom would be eliminated from death.
It is really a season for radiant uplifting. By
means of the love that follows the spirit of a
friend into his higher life, all who love him are
in some measure lifted into it.

Death is, in fact, a relative term, and sometimes a typical one. The apostle speaks to

us of being dead in trespasses and sins and alive in righteousness. "She that liveth in pleasure is dead while she liveth," — pleasure being used, not as a synonym of joy or of happiness, but of the senses and the material world. In fact life, in its true sense, is simply another name for spirituality. So much spirituality, so much life. To have spiritual force, — that is the one all-important thing. That alone is immortal. Spiritual force is the persistence of energy through whatever changes of outward form. A man may go out on the street in morning or evening dress, in a carriage or on foot, — he is the same individual in whatever external guise. So the spiritual man persists, whether clothed in a physical or a spiritual body. The difference is in the two environments that attend each form.

What is death? It is simply to enter on the correspondence with a higher condition of environment. Surely, there is nothing terrifying or sad in that. It is the entering on entirely new conditions. To some extent one enters on new conditions in removing from one country to another; the only difference between such a change as this and the change called death being that with the former the environment continues to be with visible and tangible things, while with the latter it is with spiritual things. To the spiritual being, however, these are probably as visible and tangible as is the material world to us; or, at least, as plastic to its powers. We see death, fractionally, about us every day. If a man is blind, or deaf, he is by so much dead, as regards normal sight or hearing. The eye and the ear no longer correspond to the environment.

There is such universal sorrow and suffering caused by the event we call death that it may well enlist the noblest energies of the mind to confront and analyze this event. We find a man like Mr. Howells — a man of culture and of a high order of talent — saying that he does not know how a world in which death occurs can be a happy one. Though we all profess the faith of the Christian, we meet death with a terror and grief that is pagan.

17

We reiterate our belief, and yet sorrow even as
those without hope. We drape ourselves in
black and close our homes to the sunshine.
We sit in gloom, if not in despair. We communicate and tacitly enforce sadness and
gloom on every one with whom we come in
contact. Is this a true attitude to take
toward death? Is it an attitude worthy an
immortal being? Is not all this tide of
anguish as unnecessary as it is unworthy?
and is it not simply the result of unawakened
spiritual faculties? We go about blind and
deaf to the spiritual world that is all around
us; and thus we fail to recognize those finer
forces with which we might co-operate.

Can we not more clearly, even more simply,
conceive of this truth? A human being is
potentially a spiritual being. He is a spirit
temporarily clothed in a physical body for the
purpose of gaining a certain phase of experience
through contact with the world of matter, —
as a youth is in college for a certain period to
gain a special experience and development, and,
having fulfilled this purpose, goes on and out

into the larger world. What would we think
of his fellow-students — still under-graduates
— who should regard this occasion of parting
as one of sorrow or despair? The spiritual
man having gained a given experience in the
material world, ceases to correspond with the
physical organism, and withdraws to the plane
of life just beyond this one. This is what
we call death. The temporal body is left
behind. "There is a natural body and there
is a spiritual body." The natural body is left
here, and it soon disintegrates. The soul is
now in its spiritual body and an inhabitant of
the spiritual world. But this is not another
place, only another view. We, too, are in-
habitants of the spiritual world to just the
degree in which we can live the spiritual life
and develop our spiritual perceptions. To
just the degree in which we achieve spirituality do we continue to enjoy the companionship of those in the spiritual body, and to
co-operate with them, and be co-operated with
by them, in our own work and endeavors. In
the right view there is no loss, no sadness, no

trial, no grief. On the contrary, there is, in
any true view of death, exaltation, peace, joy
and a new reinforcement of love, of courage
of higher energy. "I had relations in the
unseen," Mrs. Browning makes Aurora Leigh
say in explanation of her early life. We all
have relations in the unseen, — relations of
friendship, counsel, and guidance, relations
with whom we may be in constant and unmistakable communion.

"With what body do they come?" There
is a natural body and there is a spiritual body.
Spirit is always embodied. Casting off the
natural, it assumes the spiritual body — a
finer and an ethereal counterpart of the natural
one. The specific work a man has been doing
here he can carry on with increased power and
energy from the higher plane. To regard
death in the sense of effacement from partici-
pation in the energies of life is pagan and not
Christian. The change is an event *in* life, as
going to another country may be, save that it
involves a greater individual change. The
person becomes *more alive.* He achieves a

larger spirituality, and only so far as one lives in the spirit does he truly live at all. All physical activity is the manifestation of the spirit. Withdraw the spirit and we have — a dead body. Not a finger can *it* move of itself, not an eyelid can *it* lift, after the informing spirit has gone. So when we talk of spiritual life we talk of all the life there is. When it is controlled by high purpose, and lived in constant receptivity to the divine life, it is noble and great; in proportion as it lapses from the aspiration after the divine is it ignoble or degraded.

"What is man?" questioned Prof. Benjamin Peirce. "What a strange union of matter and of mind! A machine for converting material into spiritual force! A soul imprisoned in a body! The body is needed to hold souls apart and to preserve their independence, as well as for conversation and mutual sympathy. The body is the vocal instrument through which the soul communicates with other souls, with its past self, and even, perhaps, with its God. The soul which

leaves this earthly body still requires incor-
poration." '

The phenomena called "Spiritualism" is of
no special importance, even when it is genuine, as some proportion of it undoubtedly is.
It is, at best, incidental. "The witness is
within," as Whittier well says. Some part of
it is fraud; some part of it is inconsequential;
but occasionally, under peculiarly good conditions, there are incidents of significance.

Miss Farmer (the daughter of Prof. Moses
G. Farmer, the noted electrician) recently received the following message, signed Phillips
Brooks, on a slate which she herself held on a
table in full sunlight. Without visible hands
the pencil wrote : —

"I hope I shall never be spoken of, or thought
of again, as dead. I have come into a most remarkable condition of life. We are the same indi-
vidualities in and out of the body. I am always
glad to write a word in testimony of my continued
life."

The chirography bears a very striking resem-
blance to that of Bishop Brooks. The line, "I

have come into a most remarkable condition
of life," is like that of a great intelligence
realizing the marvellous richness of a new
phase of being; and the expression, "I am
always glad," was always that of his own
gracious words in response to any request.

This is probably the most significant message that was ever believed to be received
from the higher plane of life beyond death.
It is offered here merely as a fact that has
occurred, and one which invites fair consideration. That this slate writing is done without human hands is true. One morning, in
full sunlight, four pair of slates were being
written on, all at once, lying on top of the table,
no one touching them. If this were the work
of the subjective self, it was certainly very marvellous. It seems, indeed, more marvellous
to believe that some force outside our recognition can go from us to produce such results,
than it does to believe the simple and natural
truth that those in the life just beyond this
do the writing. The nature of the messages
should be a determining factor in this specula-

tive problem; and that they are not is a puzzling fact. For the most part, as every one knows· who has made any investigations at all into the speculative domain of psychical phenomena, — for the most part the messages are vague and without specific value. The question of phenomena is, however, one of such vast proportions, — one that could by no means be justly approached without the citation of masses of instances and facts, — that it will not here be entered upon. It is not an essential question. "My idea of heaven," says Emerson, " is that there is no melodrama in it at all; that it is wholly real."

To him who aspires to live the life of spirituality nothing can be of less significance than spiritual phenomena. Perhaps it may be added that to him who aspires and endeavors to live the life of spirituality nothing can be of more intense interest than spiritual and occult phenomena. This were sometime a paradox; yet the experience of every thoughtful person can hardly fail to corroborate and explain it himself. There has been much said, from the

ignorant to the most learned, about *proving*
immortality. No better reply to this suggestion could be made than that in the words of
Rev. O. B. Frothingham, who said : " The
proof of immortality is the feeling of immortal
desires. The pledge of the kingdom is the
undying hope of the kingdom." Certainly the
pledge and the proof of immortality lie wholly
in the daily life. Immortality is not a theory,
but an experience. If one is not immortal
to-day he can hardly expect to be so in a
thousand years. Immortality is not a mere
possible state in a vague future after the event
we call death; it is the condition of being
spiritually alive in the present. To be considerate, just, and sympathetic; to hold, every
day and every hour, the opportunities of usefulness as a priceless privilege; to be generous
rather than selfish; responsive rather than
indifferent; to be actively loving and outgoing rather than passively tolerant or careless,
— this is to be immortal now. The life of the
spirit is the life of immortality, whether it
is lived in the physical body or after death

in the spiritual body. Immortality is not a locality, but a condition ; and the question, Shall we be immortal ? is much more truly asked when changed to the form : *Are* we immortal ? If immortality were so cheap and poor a thing that its evidence must rest on any conceivable kind of phenomena, genuine or not, — then it would be too poor and cheap a thing to be worth discussing. Its great truth is the one eternal truth of life. It is true that immortality is the most important concern of humanity ; but it is *because* it is a question of life — of the daily living, of the present spiritual condition, that it is important. All that is spiritual is indestructible. It undergoes changes of form, of condition, of environment, but it is the persistence of energy and is never lost.

All that is material, that is physical, is perishable. Therefore, some men are more immortal than others. Emerson was more immortal, all through his life in this world, than is the man who lives almost entirely in the mere physical life of the senses. Immortality is a species of conquest in spiritual domain. The more one transmutes the material into the spiritual, the more immortal he becomes, the more hold he has on immortality, — just as the more cultivated and thoughtful a man becomes, the more hold has he on literature, and thought, and all the intellectual world of achievement.

It seems to be a fact that when the spirit leaves the physical body and is endowed with its spiritual body and is in the more spiritual world — where the physical has been cast off and left behind — that his fitness for entering into all the activities and enjoyments of that life must depend on the degree of spirituality that he has achieved. He comes into a world where the law of achievement is not competition and selfishness, but love and generosity; where he only that loseth his life shall find it; where the current coin is peace, joy, love, holiness. In so much greater measure, then, as he has developed those qualities before the change of death is he fitted to enter an immortal life and is he immortal. Let a man

be suddenly placed in a foreign city whose
language he cannot speak, with whose laws
and customs he is totally unfamiliar, and although he may manage to exist, he certainly
is not in a condition of sufficient harmony
with his environment to enable him to be
particularly useful or happy. It would only
be as he acquires familiarity and comes into
natural, spontaneous sympathy with his surroundings that he grows to be in harmony
with the life. But if before his arrival he
had been familiar with its language, its literature, its customs, and laws; if he were prepared to appreciate and enjoy its treasures of
art, or learning, or its social qualities, obviously he would be far more a resident, and
not an alien, in its midst; obviously he would
be far happier.

Does not the analogy hold good in comparison to the state beyond death and the
achievement of the qualities that survive the
death and decay of the physical body?

Now to hear from one's friends in Berlin or
Calcutta or Australia is an interesting fact;

but if there were no cables or postal service, it would not alter the fact of their existence in Berlin or in Australia.

May it not be thus in regard to communication between those beyond death and those of us this side of death? That the tipping of a table, a rap, the utterances of a trance medium, even a communication on a slate written without human hands or any visible agency, — a thing that is simply a fact and which is the most marvellous of any so-called "manifestations," — even that and all other species of phenomena, while they are undoubtedly, sometimes, genuine, are at the best only interesting and never essential. Immortality is a life. If one would be immortal let him live immortally now. "We have an indemnity only in the moral and intellectual reality to which we aspire. That is immortal, and we only through that."

"With what body do they come?" With the spiritual body, which is the refined and ethereal counterpart of the body we know here. They are about us in the simple, natural way. "The life which we are living now is more aware than we know of the life which is to come," said Phillips Brooks, and added: "Death, which separates the two, is not, as it has been so often pictured, like a great thick wall. It is rather like a soft and yielding curtain, through which we cannot see, but which is always waving and trembling with the impulses that come out of the life which lies upon the other side of it."

The fact of clairvoyance is one as well established as that of hypnotism. The clairvoyant sees and describes spiritual forms. There is no longer any reasonable doubt of this. Still deeper than proof is intuition. The soul is ceaselessly expectant. "On warm June mornings in country lanes, with sweet pine odors wafted in the breeze which sighs through the branches," writes Dr. John Fiske, "with cloud-shadows flitting over far-off blue mountains, while little birds sing their love-songs and golden-haired children weave garlands of wild roses; or when in the solemn twilight we listen to wondrous harmonies of

Beethoven and Chopin that stir the heart like voices from an unseen world, — at such times one feels that the profoundest answer which science can give to our questionings is but a superficial answer after all. At these moments, when the world seems fullest of beauty, one feels most strongly that it is but the harbinger of something else, — that the ceaseless play of phenomena is no mere sport of Titans, but an orderly scene, with its reason for existing, its —

(One divine, far-off event
To which the whole creation moves.) "

The entire universe is, indeed, vocal with its intimations of immortality.

*   *   *   *   *

Pure Lilies " I muse on joys that will not cease,
of Eternal   Pure spaces clothed in living beams;
Peace.   Pure lilies of eternal peace,
               Whose odors haunt my dreams."

The secret of eternal peace is to live in the spirit. " Let this mind be in you that is in Christ Jesus," said the apostle, and that mind was elsewhere defined by him as being love,

joy, peace, and righteousness. All these
qualities naturally follow large and generous
interests, affections, and hopes. Happiness
is not the result of possessions; it is the result of a wide range of interests; of that spiritual attitude that takes the good of others to
be its own, that is glad in the universal gladness, and that enters, by rejoicing, into universal progress. To hold true to noble use
whatever resources we may have is to constantly increase and enlarge them. Life is a
trust. It is the most priceless, the most infinitely valuable of possessions, — a gift of rare
powers and unlimited resources, to be used
for the benefit of others, and thus, in the truest way, for one's self. One only lives for
himself — in the best way — when he lives for
others. "Herein is my Father glorified, that
ye bear much fruit; so shall ye be my disciples," said the Christ. To "bear much
fruit" is to live in the widest relations with
human life; to render the service needed at
the moment, not counting the cost; to give
the gift that is needed, though it leave one's

own hands empty. For spiritual treasure is infinite, and to him who lives in the spirit the supply is sure. And *only* he who scattereth, increaseth. Not to scatter it wantonly, selfishly, and thoughtlessly, but in meeting every real need that appeals to us with the very best that is in our power, — this is to live in the spirit, and thus be a partaker of all the infinite and boundless riches of the Lord. This infinite store is precipitated, so to speak, in material forms that correspond with material needs. Mr. Howells, once in writing on generosity of life, represented it after the likeness of a hunter whose family were dependent for food on the results of his quest by day; and that if on the homeward journey he encountered a starving brother and gave him of his store, his own family would, perhaps, needs go hungry because of this generosity. But this bears no analogy to human life, for human life is divine life, and is not limited to the animal basis. We are spiritual beings, living in a spiritual world, and formed to partake of spiritual resources.

18

If one gives five dollars to meet a genuine
need that appeals to him, — a need which, evidently, in the working of Providence, it is his
business and not that of some one else to
meet, — he is not thereby simply five dollars the
poorer. Instead, by responding to the spiritual
call, he has entered into the spiritual life and
is made a partaker of the kingdom. He has
forged the magnetic link that admits him to
the chain of divine blessings. He that "*doeth
the will*" — it is he who is admitted into the
kingdom. We talk much — and we can never
talk too much — of the work of the Lord.
But the Lord works through human means.
It is the one highest privilege of the spirit in
human form to be a co-worker with the divine
spirit. The Lord does not miraculously drop
a loaf of bread, or a ton of coal, or clothing, or
furniture into an impoverished household, precipitated through the air like the legendary
communications of Madame Blavatsky; but he
puts it into the heart and mind of the neighbor
and friend to go and provide that load of
coal, and the food and the clothing, and thus

not impoverish his own stores, but, instead, by entering into the diviner life of the spirit, make himself, by so much, a partaker in that life.

To him who lives in the spirit all doors are open; all resources are his. There, alone, is the secret of achievement, of joy all-abounding. We live encompassed round about with the great cloud of witnesses. Along the lines of insight and sympathy divine resources pass. Great interests insure great joys. To have spiritual force, — that is *to live*. In this divineness of life the strength of each becomes the strength of all, and all are conjoined in the love of the Father.

Herein is peace attained; nor is peace a merely passive and negative state. It is the inflorescence of courage, wisdom, and love. It is the state of the most intense illumination. Peace is just as possible in this part of life as in that which lies beyond death. The great fallacy of all religious teaching has been the postponement of all active and essential consequences to the life that follows death; this

part of life being held to be a " vale of tears,"
a mere passage-way to the grave, in which
nothing that transpired was of any particular
consequence save as it affected that next life
to come. This is as idle as it would be for
the student in preparatory schools to feel that
his work and achievements there day after
day were too insignificant to dwell upon, and
that only when he entered college would study
and its results assume any real value. When
Phillips Brooks sounded that clarion call to
the true life — "*Be such a man, live such a
life, that if every man were such as you and
every life a life like yours, this earth would
be paradise,*" when he condensed into those
few wonderful words the entire essence of the
Christian life, he revealed the sacredness of
the present moment, the eternal significance
of the passing hour.

And these words offer such an inspiring
vision to one who wakens to them in the
morning. They should be set in an illumi-
nated motto and hung where the eye could
rest upon them first on waking. It is a call

to the Ideal, and to an ideal that may be increasingly realized.

The initial step to its realization is the regulation of one's thoughts; and perhaps the most difficult thing in regard to this is not always one's own thoughts, but those of others that thrust upon him their expression. When a caller comes bringing an atmosphere of fretful discontent, of jealous, spiteful, petty comment on mutual friends or acquaintances, and invades harmony with jar and annoyance, — the supreme test comes then. Yet surely even here the ideal must be to hold one's self so positively in the divine atmosphere of the higher thought that its quality shall not be affected by evil and discord without.

The power of thought is the one supreme potency of life. To learn to control this absolutely would be to hold in one's own volition the entire direction and creation of all that goes to make up the sum of living; for a sufficiently intense power of thought would be that force of spirituality which even overcomes

and annuls past karma. There is embodied
an actual truth in these words : —

"It is said that the people are poor; this is
equivalent to saying that they do not think. Let
them think and they will cease to be poor. I do
not mean poor in spirit and in moral qualities; I
mean that they will cease to be poor in purse.
The power to think guarantees wealth. Or,
rather, a finer and truer expression of this idea is,
that thought in itself and of itself does really
create a man's external conditions; it can make
him poor, or it can make him rich; it can mort-
gage his home and turn him on the street to
starve, or it can build a palace over his head that
shall be his very own for all time. . . .

"Thought can be made productive of wealth on
a higher plane than this. It possesses a power *of
itself* that nothing can resist when led forth in
proper channels. . . . The kind of wealth obtained in selfish competition does not stay; and if
it did, it would be an impediment rather than a
help on the upward road to *permanent power;*
that power which means *freedom;* the perfect
liberation of the mind from all anxiety. Only
that is wealth which liberates; only that is
wealth in which the mind finds expansion, room

for growth, and time to follow the enticements of the ideal.

"Mental science — the true science of mind, and its almost infinite power — is the only study in the world that will or can teach the people how to become rich on a plane above the present competitive one. The producers of this world may succeed in getting what they call their rights, and may obliterate the tyranny of capital as controlled by syndicates and rings, and yet be no nearer the freedom of true riches than they were before ; they will still remain in the arena of dreadful conflict by which riches are now acquired. They will be no more free than they are now. There is no freedom but by the ascension from *matter to mind ;* an ascension that the world in the aggregate has not the faintest conception of ; an ascension only beginning to be understood by the students of mental power.

"The only hope of the race to-day is in the cultivation of the ideal faculties. It is these faculties — rudimentary as yet in nine-tenths of the people — that hold the prophecy of all future growth."

The hour of the Ideal has struck, and its silver chimes vibrate throughout the world,

The age of spirit is upon us; the age in which, after ages of evolutionary progress, man asserts his birthright as a spirit, dwelling in a spiritual world, and controlled by and controlling spiritual forces. Dreams and ideals are his material; visions are the feeders and creators of his achievements.

To absolutely banish an evil and inharmonious thought; to close the door to envy, detraction, unkindness, self love; to utterly bar out resentment toward any human being, no matter what the cause; to hold one's life as, primarily, between himself and the Lord; to rejoice in the good and to be glad in the gladness of others, — this, surely, is the key to that state which would make earth heaven, and bring to every life the lilies of eternal peace.

There can be no peace where there is not serenity. There can be no serenity where all one's belongings and materials are in chaos and confusion. The Christian life certainly begins with harmonious conditions, and this is a truth that all who live in the high pressure of this age need to emphasize to themselves.

For this pressure is simply enormous. How to reconcile the demands of life is a problem that confronts us all. One has his specific work to do; he requires the collateral margin of leisure for thought concerning it, for without this quiet daily concentration of thought no work can prosper, whether it be art or commerce, science or traffic. One needs, too, due time for reading, for study, and for personal care. But there is not only the world of society, so called, but that inner and dearer world of his personal friends; those with whom he, indeed, takes sweet counsel, and whose companionship offers him perpetual sympathy and stimulus. To say he has "no time" for his friends is to cut off the sweetest resources of life. And still there are only twenty-four hours to a day and seven days to the week.

The problem is peculiarly complicated for women, who are all, more or less, in a transition stage. They take upon themselves everything that a woman ever did, and a large share of the things the woman of the past

never dreamed of regarding. Great need
hath she of that mind "which is in Christ
Jesus," — of achieving within herself that self-
control, harmony, and sweetness that shall be
love, and joy, and peace. Thus, only, can
she command the mental conditions for her
work.

To let one's self degenerate into the conditions of fume and fret and worry is to drift
into the infinite current of jar and discord,
where everything goes wrong. To hold fast
to serenity — to give one's self to Jesus, —
daily, hourly, in perpetual consecration and
communion, is to enter the magnetic current
of joy and peace and infinite energy, and
command the conditions for the noblest
success, — that of character as well as of
achievement.

Religion is a life or it is nothing. Theology
is another matter, and creeds and views have
their adherents and advocates ; but religion is
psychic science, the knowledge of the soul, the
knowledge of its capabilities, its powers, its
methods of unfoldment. To give one's self to

Jesus! The good old evangelical phrase comprehends all the possibilities of divineness of life.

To give one's self to Jesus is a life. We hear much of a man's giving himself to art, to literature, to science, to business, to this or that specialty of pursuit. The phrase is a clear one, and carries its complete significance. To give one's self to Jesus is not *one* of these phrases, but comprehends and makes complete each and all of them. A man cannot give himself to art, for instance, and to business at one and the same time. But the man who does not give himself to Jesus cannot successfully give himself to art or to commerce, to science or scholarship. " In Him we live and move and have our being." In Him is that larger life in which all modes and pursuits and purposes find their conditions and fulfilment.

And to give one's self to Jesus implies perfection of detail. We talk of trivial details, but none are really unimportant. Order is said to be heaven's first law. The definition is none too high. Order, neatness, and accuracy are the first conditions of success in any undertaking or enterprise. A nervous, hurried, and flustered state of mind is simply fatal to any good work.

The present is a period of time increasingly charged with spiritual magnetism. We hear about disastrous times and misfortunes in affairs; but the deeper truth is that no such fortunate and beautiful time has ever been known before, because this is the highest point reached in the evolution of all civilization. The highest results yet known of spiritual development and of the accumulation of spiritual force are in the world to-day. For those who are in sympathetic accord with this it is the most fortunate and the most beautiful time imaginable; a time of prosperity, of radiant happiness, of the utmost sweetness of satisfying response. Almost has the gulf between spirit and matter been bridged when an image intently held in the mind can be photographed from the eye; when the newly invented thought-machine gives a permanent record of mental processes, recording thought at any speed, transmuting the magnetic vibrations to a visible message. Julius Emmner, of Washington, D. C., the inventor of the long-distance telephone, has at last perfected this marvellous instrument. Electricity is the motive power and chemistry produces the record. We are here and now in a spiritual world, ruled by spiritual forces; and just in proportion as one lives in the spirit, — lives unselfishly, with ardor, and purpose, and enthusiasm, — does he live in the invisible world and find his daily consciousness of heaven. The scene of action, in those years, is transferred to a higher plane than heretofore; but to all who rise to that plane the years will be transfigured in loveliness. The time for doubt, defeat, depression, and despair has gone by. Joy, sweetness, and exaltation are now the daily manna showered upon all who will lift up their hearts and partake. The very atmosphere thrills with this new and resistless energy, this divine enthusiasm.

The law of success is to expect success.
Thus alone is one within its magnetism. It
is, too, a serious loss — a fatal one, indeed —
to fail in realization of the infinite store of joy,
health, prosperity, happiness, that is in the
universe. If an individual were under the
delusion that the supply of air was limited,
and that he must breathe very sparingly and
subsist on the minimum of oxygen a day that
he might thereby save and economize on it so
that it should last his lifetime, it could hardly
be more idle than the prevailing idea that one
must hoard by and save and "lay by" as a
provision for future years. The one best provision for the future is the best possible use
of the present. The daily manna is typical
of the supplies of life. They who ate the
manna each day and trusted to its renewal
on the morrow were supplied; but they who
hoarded it found it unfit for use the next day.
There is really no question but that if all
humanity could live on the plane of a higher
energy of life, taking no thought as to what
they should eat or drink or wherewithal

they should be clothed, — according to the
literal words of Jesus, — they would at once
liberate a new and wholly undreamed of
source of supplies, and eliminate from life
much of the present irksomeness of material
detail. The happy conditions of life in exhilaration and joy are to be had on the same
terms as its burden and anxiety.

It may be urged that one cannot abandon
anxiety at will, and this is true. But he can
desire to abandon it, and thus place himself
in the current of receptivity to the uplifting
currents of thought, and they will flow in.
Everything that is lovely and good abounds.
The supply of the highest is infinite.

The supreme lesson that the experiences of
this life teach are these : —

That there are things in life of importance and
of no importance ; that there is the essential
and the non-essential. It is not important or
essential to a man to possess the outer luxuries of life ; the quality of a rug, the richness
of upholstery, even the luxuries of art, — one
can live without. He comes to realize that

a good dinner is not an important factor in his enjoyment; that what he shall eat, drink, or wherewithal be clothed, is all, at best, a minor matter; but that it is of the greatest importance that he be honest, truthful, just, considerate, generous, and courteous. He thus separates the essential from the non-essential.

No prelate of the church, robed in priestly canonicals, ministering at the altar, has upon him any more the responsibility to live the divine life; nor has he any more entirely the opportunity to live it than has the railway magnate in his official sanctum, the merchant in his store, the saleswoman at the counter; than any man or woman in any art, profession, or industry. *Religion is a life and not a ceremony.*

But the beautiful spirit that goes out reacts and produces its corresponding effects on the visible plane. No one can be unhappy who is filled with interest in the happiness of others. Gloom and depression are thereby swept away, and vanish in the radiant atmosphere. Life is a beautiful thing to live when lived in the spirit. It is exalted and joyful. To carry the "glad tidings" is the highest privilege to any individual, and is the privilege open to all, and one that multiplies with every advantage that is taken of it. We are entering on a new age of spiritualization, and to live in the spirit is the only means by which we may enter into its highest harmony.

One of the mystics has written :—

"The will of God is the alchemic crucible, and the dross which is cast therein is matter.

"And the dross shall become pure gold, seven times refined, even perfect spirit.

"It shall leave behind it nothing, but shall be transformed into the divine image.

"For it is not a new substance, but its alchemic polarity is changed and it is converted.

"But except it were gold in its true nature it could not be resumed into the aspect of gold.

"And except matter were spirit it could not revert to spirit.

"To make gold, the alchemist must have gold.

"But he knows that to be gold which others take to be dross.

19

"Cast. thyself into the will of God, and thou shalt become as God.

"For thou art God if thy will be the Divine will.

"This is the great secret; it is the mystery of redemption."

Here then is the key to abiding peace. Cast thyself into the will of God. This is the crucible where all the forces are remoulded and prepared to exert creative power. Latent possibilities thus come to their development and enter on their purpose. As all matter is transparent to the Roentgen rays, so is all achievement held in solution by spiritual force, — a force infinitely more intense than electricity. When Jesus said to his disciples, "All things are yours," the words were not a mere trick of phrasing. They assert a definite truth. All things belong to every one who has cast himself into the will of God. The penetrating power of the ultra-violet light is as nothing to the penetrating power of spiritual energy. Humanity will enter on its birthright when it comes into the full realization of the mystic truth that all things are added to him who has sought first the kingdom of righteousness. In that kingdom is the storehouse of infinite treasure from which all who enter may draw freely. Then shall mankind come to the supreme inheritance of that last divine gift of which Jesus, the Christ, said: "Peace I give to you; my peace I give unto you. Let not your hearts be troubled, neither let them be afraid."

THE END.

Printed in Great Britain
by Amazon